WEAVING IT TOGETHER

2

Milada Broukal

Glendale Community College

Heinle & Heinle Publishers
A Division of Wadsworth, Inc.
Boston, Massachusetts 02116 U.S.A.

The publication of *Weaving It Together 2* was directed by members of the Heinle & Heinle ESL Publishing Team:

Erik Gundersen, **Editorial Director**
Susan Mraz, **Marketing Manager**
Kristin Thalheimer, **Production Editor**

Also participating in the publication of this program were:

Publisher: Stanley J. Galek
Editorial Production Manager: Elizabeth Holthaus
Associate Editor: Lynne Telson Barsky
Project Manager: Hockett Editorial Service
Manufacturing Coordinator: Mary Beth Lynch
Photo Coordinator: Martha Leibs-Heckly
Interior Designer: Winston • Ford Visual Communications
Illustrators: Libby Barrett, Brian Orr, James Edwards
Cover Illustrator: Lisa Houck
Cover Designer: Judy Ziegler

Photo Credits (page numbers are given in boldface):
UPI/Bettmann—**1** (Chaplin), **56**, **86**. UPI/Bettmann Newsphotos—**1** (McEnroe, Monroe, McCartney), **65** (Wonder), **94**. The Bettmann Archive—**1** (Einstein), **74**, **82** (Lincoln), **83** (King, Keller, Shelley), **136**. Archive Photos—**1** (Da Vinci), **82** (Edison, Mozart), **105**. Ulrike Welsch—**14**, **83** (Mother Theresa). FPG International—**25**. Four by Five—**26**. Georg Gerster, Comstock—**47**. Frank Edwards, Fotos International, Archive Photos—**65** (Chung, Cruise). David R. Frazier—**66**. Michael Grecco, Stock, Boston—**85**. Eric Neurath, Stock, Boston—**114**. Russ Kinne, Comstock—**125**, **126**.

Heinle & Heinle Publishers is a division of Wadsworth, Inc.

Manufactured in the United States of America

Library of Congress Cataloging-in-Publication Data

Broukal, Milada.
    Weaving it together 2 / Milada Broukal.
        p.   cm.
    ISBN 0-8384-3977-2
    1. English language—Textbooks for foreign speakers.   I. Title.
    II. Title: Weaving it together two.
    PE1128.B715   1993   92-43932
    428.2′4—dc20   CIP

CONTENTS

4　Delicacies　36

Unit 3:　Customs and Traditions

5　How Do They Bathe?　48

6　Unusual Marriage Ceremonies　56

Unit 4: Famous People

 7 **Louis Braille**   **66**

8 **The World's Most Unusual Millionaire**   **74**

TO THE TEACHER

Rationale

Weaving It Together, Book 2 is the second in a three-book series that integrates reading and writing skills for students of English as a second or foreign language. The complete program includes the following:

> **Book 1 . . . Beginning level**

> **Book 2 . . . High beginning level**

> **Book 3 . . . Intermediate level**

The central premise of *Weaving It Together* is that reading and writing are interwoven and inextricable skills. Good readers write well; good writers read well. With this premise in mind, *Weaving It Together* has been developed to meet the following objectives:

1. To combine reading and writing through a comprehensive, systematic, and engaging process designed to effectively integrate the two.
2. To provide academically bound students with serious and engaging multicultural content.
3. To promote individualized and cooperative learning within the moderate to large-sized class.

Over the past few years, a number of noted researchers in the field of second language acquisition have written about the serious need to effectively integrate reading and writing instruction in both classroom practice and materials development. *Weaving It Together* is, in many ways, a response to this need.

Barbara Kroll, for example, talks of teaching students to read like writers and write like readers (1993). She notes: "It is only when a writer is able to cast himself or herself in the role of a reader of the text under preparation that he or she is able to anticipate the reader's needs by writing into the text what he or she expects or wants the reader to take out from the text." Through its systematic approach to integrating reading and writing, *Weaving It Together* teaches ESL and EFL students to understand the kinds of interconnections between reading and writing which they need to make in order to achieve academic success.

Linda Lonon Blanton's research focuses on the need for second language students to develop authority, conviction, and certainty in their writing. She believes that students develop strong writing skills in concert with good reading skills. Blanton writes: "My experience tells me that empowerment, or achieving this certainty and authority, can be achieved only through performance—through the act of speaking and writing about texts, through developing individual responses to texts." (1992)

For Blanton, as for Kroll and others, both reading and writing must be treated as composing processes. Effective writing instruction must be integrally linked with effective reading instruction. This notion is at the heart of *Weaving It Together*.

Organization of the Text

Weaving It Together, Book 2, contains seven thematically organized units, each of which includes two interrelated chapters. Each chapter begins with a reading, moves on to a set of activities designed to develop critical reading skills, and culminates with a series of interactive writing exercises.

Each chapter contains the following sequence of activities:

1. **Pre-reading questions:** Each chapter is introduced with a page of photographs or drawings accompanied by a set of discussion questions. The purpose of the pre-reading questions is to prepare students for the reading by activating their background knowledge and encouraging them to call on and share their experiences.

2. **Reading:** Each reading is a high-interest, non-fiction passage related to the theme of the unit. Selected topics include Right Brain or Left Brain?, Unusual Marriage Ceremonies, and Laws About Children.

3. **Vocabulary:** The vocabulary in bold type in each reading passage is practiced in the vocabulary exercise which follows the passage. The vocabulary items introduced and practiced provide a useful source for students when they are writing their own paragraphs on the same theme.

4. **Comprehension:** There are two types of comprehension exercises: The first, *Looking for Main Ideas*, concentrates on a general understanding of the reading. This exercise may be done after a first silent reading of the text. Students can reread the text to check answers. The second comprehension exercise, *Looking for Details*, concentrates on developing skimming and scanning skills.

5. **Discussion:** Students may work in small or large groups and interact with each other to discuss questions that arise from the reading. These questions ask students to relate their experiences to what they have learned from the reading. The last question in the *Discussion* section provides a natural transition to the section entitled *Model Paragraph*.

6. **Model paragraph:** This paragraph is written by an international student whose writing skills are slightly more advanced than those of the writers who will use *Weaving It Together, Book 2*. The paragraph follows the general rhetorical form of North American academic prose, and provides a natural preparation for the more discreet points taught in the organizing section.

7. **Organizing:** With each of the fourteen readings a different aspect of paragraph organization is developed. These aspects include paragraph structure, transitions, and rhetorical devices which the student will use to develop his or her own paragraph. Exercises following the points taught reinforce the organizational techniques introduced.

8. **Pre-writing:** Brainstorming and clustering techniques are presented and practiced in this section of the text. These help students activate their background knowledge before they start to write.

9. **Developing an outline:** Using the ideas they have generated in the pre-writing section, students put together an outline for their writing. This outline acts as a ''framework'' for the work ahead.

10. **Writing a rough draft:** A rough draft of the paragraph is written. *Weaving It Together* encourages students to write several rough drafts, since writing is an ongoing process.

11. **Revising your draft using the checklist:** Students can work on their own or with a partner to check their paragraphs, and make any necessary alterations. Teachers are encouraged to add any further points they consider important to the checklist provided.

12. **Editing your paragraph:** In this section, students are encouraged to work with a partner or their teacher to correct spelling, punctuation, vocabulary and grammar.

13. **Writing your final copy:** Students prepare the final version of the paragraph.

Journal Writing

In addition to the projects and exercises in the book, I strongly recommend that students be instructed to keep a journal in which they correspond with you. The purpose of this journal is for them to tell you how they feel about the class each day. It gives them an opportunity to tell you what they like, what they dislike, what they understand, and what they don't understand. By having students explain what they have learned in the class, you can discover whether or not they understand the concepts taught.

Journal writing is effective for two major reasons. First, since this type of writing focuses on fluency and personal expression, students always have something to write about. Second, journal writing can also be used to identify language concerns and troublespots which need further review. In its finest form, journal writing can become an active dialogue between teacher and student that permits you both to learn more about your students' lives and to individualize their language instruction.

References

Blanton, Linda Lonon (1992). "Reading, Writing, and Authority: Issues in Developmental ESL." *College ESL*, 2, 11–19.

Kroll, Barbara (1993). "Teaching Writing *Is* Teaching Reading: Training the New Teacher of ESL Composition" in *Reading in the Composition Classroom* (Heinle & Heinle Publishers, Boston), 61–81.

TO THE STUDENT

This book will teach you to read and write in English. You will study readings on selected themes and learn strategies for writing a good paragraph on those themes. In the process, you will be exposed to the writings and ideas of others as well as ways of expressing your own ideas so that you can work toward writing a paragraph of approximately 150–200 words in good English.

It is important for you to know that writing well in English may be quite different from writing well in your native language. Good Chinese or Arabic writing is different from good English writing. Not only are the styles different but the organization is different too. Good Spanish organization is different from good English organization.

The processes of reading and writing are closely interconnected. Therefore, in this text we are weaving reading and writing together. I hope that the readings in this text will stimulate your interest to write, and that *Weaving It Together* will make writing in English much easier for you.

Milada Broukal

UNIT 1

Your
Personality

Chapter 1: Right Brain or Left Brain?

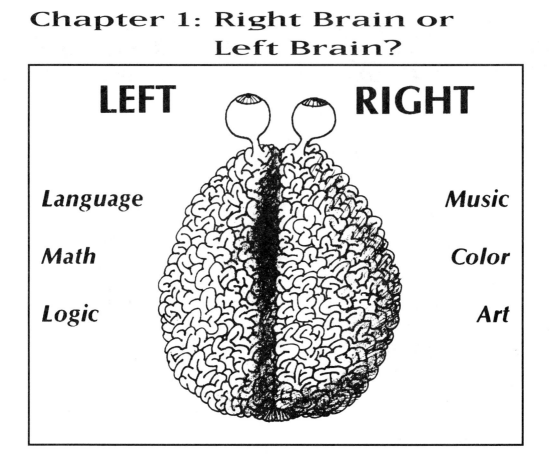

LEFT   **RIGHT**

Language   Music

Math   Color

Logic   Art

PRE-READING QUESTIONS

Discuss these questions with your classmates or teacher.

1. Do you know the names of the people in the picture on page 1?

2. What are they famous for?

3. All of them have one thing which is the same. What do you think it is?

Reading: Right Brain or Left Brain?

What do Leonardo da Vinci, Paul McCartney, Napoleon, and John McEnroe have **in common**? They are all left-handed. Today about 15 percent of the **population** is left-handed. But why are people left-handed? The answer is in the way the brain works.

The brain has two halves—the right half and the left half. The right half controls the left side of the body, and the left controls the right side of the body. So right-handed people have a strong left brain, and left-handed people have a strong right brain.

The two halves of the brain are about the same size. But each side controls different things. The left side controls language, math, and **logic**. When you **memorize** the spelling of words, or when you put things in order, you use your left side. The right side of the brain controls your love of art, color, music. It is also good at **recognizing** faces.

This does not mean that all artists are left-handed and all accountants are right-handed. There are many **exceptions**. Some right-handers have a strong right brain, and some left-handers have a strong left brain.

VOCABULARY

Complete the definitions. Circle the letter of the correct answer.

1. When two people have something which is the same, they have something _____.

   a. in order

   b. in common

2. Another word for the number of people living in a place is

   _____.

   a. faces

   b. population

3. When you think and give reasons that follow rules, you use the science of _____.

   a. logic

   b. art

4. When you remember a poem or a telephone number, you
   remember because you _____ it.
      a. memorized
      b. order

5. When you see something or someone and know what or who it is,
   you _____ it.
      a. control
      b. recognize

6. When something or someone does not belong with the others, it is
   _____.
      a. an exception
      b. a left brain

COMPREHENSION

A. Looking for the Main Ideas

Read the passage again and look for the MAIN IDEAS. Circle the letter of the correct answer.

1. People are right-handed or left-handed because of
   _____.
      a. the population
      b. the way the brain works
      c. Paul McCartney and Napoleon

2. The brain has _____.
      a. two halves
      b. two left halves
      c. two hands

3. Each side of the brain_____.
      a. likes language and math
      b. controls the same thing
      c. controls different things

B. Looking for Details

Read the passage again and look for DETAILS. Circle T if the sentence is true. Circle F if the sentence is false.

1. Fifty percent of the population is left-handed.   T F
2. The right side of the brain controls the left side of the body.   T F
3. The left side of the brain controls color.   T F
4. The right side of the brain controls art.   T F
5. All accountants are right-handed.   T F
6. When you recognize a face you are using your right brain.   T F

DISCUSSION

Discuss the answers to these questions with your classmates.

1. Do you think children should be forced to be right-handed?
2. Does the word "left" have a negative meaning in your language? Is it bad to be left-handed in your country?
3. Ask a left-handed person these questions:
   1. Are your parents left-handed?
   2. Are you left-footed?
   3. When you play tennis or some other sport, are you left-handed or right-handed?
   4. When you were a child, did people try to make you right-handed?
   5. Do you want to be right-handed?
   6. What things do you find difficult to use (scissors, can openers, doors)?
   7. Do you think you write slower than a right-handed person?

Discuss the answers you get in groups.

Paragraph Form

	Yumi Ono	
	3/3/93	
	ESL 163	
Indent	Left-handed People	Center title
	Left-handed people have many problems	
	living in a world for right-handed people. First,	
	driving a car may be a problem. All the	
Capitalize the first word in each sentence.	important things in the car are on the right. For	
	example, the ignition switch, the gear shift, and	
	the accelerator and brake are all on the right.	
	Second, using a typewriter may be a problem.	
	Typewriters are again made for right-handed	
	people and all the keys are on the right. This	
One-inch margin	includes the on-off button, carriage return,	One-inch margin
	period, comma, and other important punctuation	
	marks. In conclusion, left-handed people have to	
	work harder than right-handed people to do	
	simple things.	

Paragraph Form

You will learn how to write a good paragraph in this book. Before you start to write, it is important for you to know the requirements of a good paragraph.

Instructions on Paragraph Form

1. Use lined paper.
2. Write your name, course number, and date in the upper right-hand corner.
3. Write a title in the center of the top of the page.
4. Leave a one-inch margin on both sides of the page. Do not write in the left-hand margin.
5. Indent the first line of every paragraph. When you write by hand, indent the first line about one inch from the margin. When you type, indent the first line five spaces. In business letters you do not have to indent the first line of every paragraph.
6. Write on every other line of the paper.
7. Capitalize the first word in each sentence and end each sentence with a period.

PUNCTUATION AND CAPITALIZATION

Each sentence begins with a capital letter. Each sentence ends with a period (.). The first word after a comma (,) begins with a small letter.

There are rules for using capital letters. Here are some rules.

Capitalization Rules

1. Capitalize the first word in a sentence.

   Today about 15 percent of the population is left-handed.
2. Capitalize the pronoun **I**.

   Paul and I are left-handed.
3. Capitalize all proper nouns. Here are some proper nouns:

   Names of people and their titles:

John McEnroe	*Mr. John Smith*
Napoleon	*Dr. Mary Roberts*
Marilyn Monroe	

Names of places you can find on a map:
Verdugo Road	Times Square
Central Avenue	Canada
Lake Victoria	London, England

Names of nationalities, races, languages, and religions:
American	Hispanic
Asian	Moslem
Catholic	Arab

Names of specific organizations (schools, business):
University of California	Glendale College
Bank of America	Safeway
International Students Club	Red Cross

Names of school subjects with course numbers:
English 101	Spanish 01A

Names of days, months, and special days:
Monday	Independence Day
May	Halloween

Names of special buildings and bridges:
The White House	Golden Gate Bridge

Exercise 1

Change the small letters to capital letters where necessary.

1. st. mary's college is located in boston, massachusetts.

2. in august 1959, hawaii became the fiftieth state of the united states.

3. i hit my car on the corner of greenwood avenue and lexington.

4. maria is a student from peru. she speaks spanish, french, and italian.

5. there are no classes during christmas, easter, and thanksgiving vacation.

6. students who were buddhist, moslem, christian, and jewish all got together to help.

7. i am taking three classes this semester: english 120, spanish 1A, and business administration.

8. have you been to see the white house in washington, d.c.?

Answer the following questions with complete sentences. Use capital letters where necessary.

1. What is your full name?

   _____

2. Write the names of three other students in your class.

   _____

   _____

   _____

3. What languages do you speak?

   _____

   _____

   _____

4. Write the names of three other languages that students in your class speak.

   _____

   _____

   _____

5. Where do you come from (city and country)?

   _____

6. Write the names of five holidays that you know (in the United States or your country).

_____

_____

_____

_____

_____

7. Write the name and address of your school or college.

_____

_____

_____

8. What classes are you going to take this year?

_____

_____

_____

_____

HOW TO WRITE A TITLE

A title tells the reader the topic of the paragraph. A title is usually a word or phrase. It is not a sentence.

Remember these points:

1. Capitalize the first, last, and all important words in the title. Do not capitalize prepositions and articles.

   Exceptions: Capitalize articles that begin the title.

2. Do not underline the title.

3. Do not use a period (.), a comma (,), or quotation marks (" "). But you can use an exclamation mark (!) or a question mark (?).

Examples of titles:

Right or Left Brain?
The Importance of Having a Friend
My First Day in the United States
Learning Can Be Fun, Too!

Exercise 3

Say what is wrong with the titles below. Then write the titles in the correct way.

1. Eating In The United States Of America.

   _____

   _____

2. "Learning english Is Important."

   _____

   _____

3. I have many problems because I am living away from my family.

   _____

   _____

4. the Most Important Day Of My Life

   _____

   _____

This simple writing test will tell you.

1. Write your name on a piece of paper.
2. Did your pen point away from you when you wrote? Was your hand below the line of writing (straight writing)?
3. Did the pen point toward you? Was your hand above the line of writing (hooked writing)?

You have a strong right brain if:

1. You write straight with your left hand.
2. You write hooked with your right hand. (See picture.)

You have a strong left brain if:

1. You write straight with your right hand.
2. You write hooked with your left hand.

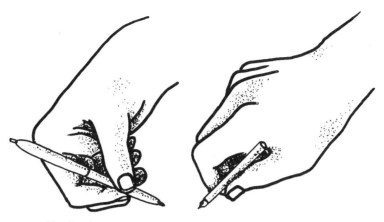

Hooked

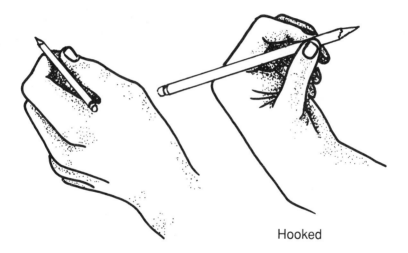

Hooked

Chapter 2: Ears and Your Character

PRE-READING QUESTIONS

Discuss these questions with your classmates or teacher.

1. Look at this face. Which part of the face tells you more about the person's character? The eyes? The mouth?

2. Look at the person's ears. What do you think the ears tell you?

3. Look at the person's mouth, nose, eyes, hair, and chin. What can you say about this person?

Reading: Ears and Your Character

The size and **shape** of your ears show your character more than any other part of the face. Other parts of the face change shape as we get older, but ears do not change their shape. They only change in size.

Reading people's character from their ears is a very old science. In **ancient** times people thought that a person with big ears had a good and **generous** character. They thought that a person with **pale**, small ears was dangerous. They also thought that the shape of the ear showed if a person was musical or not. Today, too, many people believe that the size and shape of the ear helps you know if a person is musical.

Ears are all different, and each **characteristic** has a meaning. Next time you look at a person, see if his or her ears are large, medium-sized, or small. Look at the **lobes**. Are they attached to the face? Ears that are always red mean that a person may **have a temper**, or he/she may just have high blood pressure. Ears that are always cold and pale mean that a person has a nervous character. And a big inside the ear means a person is musical.

VOCABULARY

What is the meaning of the underlined words? Circle the letter of the correct answer.

1. The size and <u>shape</u> of your ears show your character.

    a. form

    b. color

2. In <u>ancient</u> times people thought that a person with big ears had a good character.

    a. bad

    b. very old

3. A person with big ears had a good and <u>generous</u> character.

    a. giving (of help and money)

    b. orderly and neat (of things)

4. They thought a person with <u>pale</u> ears was dangerous.

    a. almost white

    b. very dark

5. Each <u>characteristic</u> has a meaning.

    a. answer

    b. special quality

6. Look at the <u>lobes</u>.

    a. top part of the ears

    b. round, fleshy part at the bottom of the ears

7. Ears that are always red mean that a person may <u>have a temper.</u>

    a. get sad suddenly

    b. get angry suddenly

COMPREHENSION

A. Looking for the Main Ideas

Circle the letter of the correct answer.

1. The size and shape of your ears show your character

    _____.

    a. more than other parts of your face

    b. as we get older

    c. because they change shape

2. Reading people's character from their ears is _____.

    a. only for music

    b. an old idea

    c. very new

3. Each characteristic of the ear _____.

    a. has no meaning

    b. has a meaning

    c. has a meaning in music

B. Looking for Details

Circle T if the sentence is true. Circle F if the sentence is false.

1. In ancient times people thought someone with big ears was dangerous.   T F

2. Today people do not believe the size and shape of the ears show if a person is musical or not.   T F

3. Cold and pale ears may mean a person has a nervous   T   F
   character.

4. A big ear means a person is musical.   T   F

5. Lobes attached to the face mean a person has high blood   T   F
   pressure.

6. Ears that are red mean a person may have a temper.   T   F

DISCUSSION

Discuss these questions with your classmates.

1. Do you think there is any truth in reading people's faces
   (physiognomy)? How reliable is it?

2. From the students in your class find out which part of the face
   helps them understand a person's character. Fill out the
   questionnaire below.

3. Discuss what shape of face, eyes, mouth, etc. shows a good character.

Name	Country	Shape of Face	Eyes	Mouth	Ears	Other

ORGANIZING

Joining Compound Sentences with *and, but, or*

A **compound sentence** is made by joining two simple sentences. These two
simple sentences are joined by a **coordinating conjunction**. In this unit we
will look at the coordinating conjunctions **and**, **but**, and **or**.

Using *and* to Join Two Sentences

We can use **and** to join two sentences that are alike or to join one
which gives extra information to the other.

Example:

Ears are all different. Each characteristic has a meaning.

Ears are all different, **and** each characteristic has a meaning.

Note: We use a comma before **and**.

Using *but* to Join Two Sentences

We can use **but** to join two sentences that give opposite information or to join a positive sentence and a negative sentence which talk about the same subject.

(+ but −)
(− but +)

Example:

Other parts of the face change as we get older. Ears do not change shape.

Other parts of the face change shape as we get older, **but** ears do not change shape.

Note: We use a comma before **but**.

Using *or* to Join Two Sentences

We can use **or** to join two sentences that give a choice or alternative.

Example:

Ears that are always red mean that a person may have a bad temper. He/she may just have high blood pressure.

Ears that are always red mean that a person may have a bad temper, **or** he/she may just have high blood pressure.

Note: We use a comma before **or**.

Note: We only use a comma with **and**, **but**, **or** in compound sentences. When we use **and**, **but**, **or** in simple sentences we do not use a comma. In a sentence **and**, **but**, **or** can join two nouns, two adjectives, two adverbs, or two verbs.

Examples:

1. Two nouns joined by **and**

   The size **and** shape of your ears show your character.
   (noun) + **(noun)**

2. Two adjectives joined by **and**

   Ears that are cold **and** pale mean a person is nervous.
   (adj) + **(adj)**

3. Two nouns joined by **or**

   A big inside cavity **or** hole means a person is musical.
   (noun) + **(noun)**

4. Two adjectives joined by **or**
   They also thought that the shape of the ear showed if a person was musical **or** not musical.
   (adj) + **(adj)**

Compare the sentences you just read with the compound sentences you have studied.

Now underline all the coordinating conjunctions and, but, *and* or *in the reading passage. Notice the punctuation with simple and compound sentences.*

Exercise 1

Join the following sentences into compound sentences with the conjunctions in parentheses. Use the correct punctuation.

1. Ears with pointed edges are unusual. They show a changeable character. (and)

   Ears with pointed edges are unusual, and they show a changeable character.

2. Large ears with sharp edges show kindness. They usually belong to people with a happy character. (and)

   _____

   _____

3. Small ears are typical of people who are sensitive. These people are often thoughtful. (and)

   _____

   _____

4. Some ears may be large. The lobes may be small. (but)

   _____

   _____

5. A full, fleshy lobe means a person is full of life and likes the good things in life. This person may also be jealous in character. (but)

   _____

   _____

Ears of Different Shapes and Sizes

Ears with pointed edges are unusual. They show a changeable character.

Large ears with sharp edges show a person is kind. This is also a happy person.

A large ear may have small lobes.

Small ears are typical of people who are sensitive. They are also thoughtful.

Some ears have thin edges. They may have no edges. People with these ears are extroverts.

Large ears show a person likes the pleasures in life. The small lobe shows self-control.

A full, fleshy lobe means a person is full of life and likes the good things in life. This person may also be jealous in character.

Ears that stick out show that the person is brave and proud. A person with these ears may like new adventures.

6. Ears that stick out show that the person is brave and proud. A person with these ears may like new adventures. (and)

_____

_____

7. Some ears have thin edges. They may have no edges. (or)

_____

_____

8. Large ears show a person likes the pleasures in life. The small lobe shows self-control. (but)

_____

_____

Exercise 2

*Write compound sentences with **and, but, and or**. Remember to write two complete sentences. Then join them with **and, but, and or**. Do not forget to punctuate.*

1. Write a sentence about a characteristic of a person's face. Use the word "and" to join your compound sentence.

   Example: My grandfather has big ears with big lobes, **and** everybody says he will live for a long time.

   _____

   _____

2. Write a compound sentence with the word "but" about a person's face.

   Example: Uncle Joe has a red face, **but** he does not have a bad temper.

   _____

   _____

3. Write a compound sentence with the word "or" about a person's face.

   Example: Tony looks pale, **or** he may be just tired.

   _____

   _____

WRITING PRACTICE

In the following exercise you will rewrite a paragraph following the rules you have learned in this unit. In Unit Two you will be writing your own paragraphs.

Exercise 3

Work alone or with a friend.

The paragraph below has some mistakes. **Rewrite _the paragraph._** **_Make sure you do these things:_**

1. Write a title.
2. Indent.
3. Join the sentences with the correct word from the parentheses.
4. Check for capital letters, periods, and commas.

> eyes are a very important part of the Face. Your eyes will tell people your real feelings. When a person smiles, check his/her eyes for smile lines (and/but) a warm expression. The lips can lie in a smile (but/and/or) the eyes cannot lie. Your pupils* get bigger or smaller. when you look at the light, they get bigger (but/and) when you look at the dark they get smaller. your pupils also get bigger when you look at something you like (and) they get smaller when you look at something you do not like. So light-colored eyes are easier to read (and/or) dark eyes are a mystery.

Exercise 4

Write your final copy of the paragraph above.

*Pupils: In the center of the colored part of your eyes, the small, black round part.

Check True or False.

1. Your brain itself does not feel any pain.

   True   False

2. Your brain weighs about one pound.

   True   False

3. A woman's brain is heavier than a man's brain.

   True   False

4. You are left-handed or right-handed from the day you are born.

   True   False

5. There are twice as many left-handed men as women.

   True   False

6. There have been no left-handed presidents in the United States.

   True   False

7. The brain works on electricity.

   True   False

UNIT 2

Food
. . . .

Chapter 3: Potatoes

PRE-READING QUESTIONS

Discuss these questions with your classmates or teacher.

1. How do you like to eat potatoes?
2. How often do you eat potatoes?
3. What do you see on the french fries in the picture?
4. What do you eat french fries with?
5. What do you see on the baked potato?
6. Which do you prefer to eat? Say why.

Reading: Potatoes

Can you **imagine** life without french fries? Potatoes are very popular today. But in the past this was not true. Potatoes grew in South America five thousand years ago. But they only became popular in other places two hundred years ago.

In the 16th century, the Spanish took the potato from South America to Europe. But the people in Europe did not like this strange vegetable. Some people thought that if you ate the potato your skin would look like the skin of a potato. Other people could not believe that you ate the underground part of the plant. So they ate the leaves **instead**. This made them sick because there is **poison** in the leaves.

In the 1800s people started to eat potatoes. In Ireland potatoes became the main food. Then, in 1845, a **disease** killed all the potatoes in Ireland. Two million people died of hunger.

Today, each country has its potato **dish**. Germans eat potato salad, and the United States has the **baked** potato. And, of course, the French **invented** french fries. Now french fries are popular all over the world. The English eat them with salt and vinegar, the French eat them with salt and pepper, and the Americans with **ketchup**.

VOCABULARY

Complete the definitions. Circle the letter of the correct answer.

1. When you have a picture in your mind about something, you

   _____

   a. imagine.

   b. grow.

2. When you want something in place of something else, you want it

   _____

   a. soon.

   b. instead.

3. A person can get sick or die if he/she takes or eats

   _____

   a. poison.

   b. salt.

4. A sickness that passes from one person to another is a

_____

    a. disease.

    b. hunger.

5. Special cooked food of one kind is called a _____

    a. salad.

    b. dish.

6. A whole potato with its skin, cooked in an oven is

_____

    a. fried.

    b. baked.

7. When you think of or make something for the first time, you

_____

    a. become.

    b. invent.

8. The tomato sauce that you usually buy in a bottle is called

_____

    a. vinegar.

    b. ketchup.

COMPREHENSION

A. Looking for the Main Ideas

Circle the letter of the best answer.

1. Potatoes are _____.

    a. popular today

    b. not popular today

    c. never popular

2. In the 16th century, people in Europe _____.

    a. liked the potato

    b. had bad skin

    c. did not like the potato

3. People started to _____.

   a. eat potatoes in the 1800s

   b. kill potatoes in the 1800s

   c. go to Ireland in the 1800s

4. French fries are _____.

   a. salt and pepper

   b. popular all over the world

   c. from Germany

B. Looking for Details

One word in each sentence is not correct. Rewrite the sentence with the correct word.

1. Potatoes grew in Europe five thousand years ago.

   _____

   _____

2. In the 18th century, the Spanish took the potato to Europe.

   _____

   _____

3. There is poison in the skin of the potato.

   _____

   _____

4. A disease killed the people in Ireland in 1845.

   _____

   _____

5. Five million people died of hunger in Ireland.

   _____

   _____

6. Germany has the baked potato.

_____

_____

7. The Americans invented french fries.

_____

_____

DISCUSSION

1. **Find out from the students in your class what the main food and drink is in their country. Fill out the questionnaire below.**

Name	Country	Main Food	Main Drink
Berta	Mexico	Tortillas	Coffee

2. **Is the main drink in your country good for you? Say why or why not.**

3. **Are there any customs related to the main food in your country?**

Now read the following paragraph written by a student. Can you guess where the student is from?

Model Paragraph

Bread

In my country, X, bread is an important part of our everyday food. When we sit down for a meal, there is always bread on the table. For breakfast, we have bread with butter or cheese. Some people have jam or olives. For lunch, we have bread with a meat or vegetable dish. Poor people eat more bread with a small piece of meat or vegetable or cheese. For example, the lunch of a worker may be a loaf of bread with some yogurt. Again at dinner, we eat bread with whatever food there is on the table. When there is rice, we have bread, too. We think that if there is no bread, there is no food.

ORGANIZING

The Topic Sentence

Underline the first sentence in the model paragraph. This is the **topic sentence.**

1. The **topic sentence** is the most important sentence in a paragraph. It tells the reader what the paragraph is about, or its main idea. The topic sentence is usually the first sentence in a paragraph. The **topic sentence** has two parts: the **topic**, and the **controlling idea**. The **topic** is the subject of your paragraph. It is what you are writing about.

Example:

Bread is an important part of our everyday food.
Topic: Bread

Circle the topic in these sentences.

1. Potatoes are good for you.
2. There are many kinds of rice.
3. The hamburger is a popular food in America.
4. People drink tea all around the world.
5. Bread is the poor man's food.

The **controlling idea** limits or controls your topic to one aspect that you want to write about.

Example:

Topic　　　　　**Controlling idea**

Rice plays an important part in some ceremonies.

or

Topic　　**Controlling idea**

Rice is a nutritious part of our diet.

A **topic** can have more than one **controlling idea**. You could write one paragraph about how rice plays an important part in some ceremonies; you could write a second paragraph about how rice is a nutritious part of our diet; and you could write a third paragraph about another aspect of rice. There are many possibilities.

Exercise 2

Underline the controlling idea in these topic sentences.

1. Bread is an important part of our diet.
2. Bread plays an important part in our religion.
3. Potatoes are easy to grow.
4. Potatoes are the basic food of the Irish.
5. French fries are popular all over the world.

2. **Topic sentences** are opinions. A simple fact cannot be a topic sentence because there is nothing more you can say about it. If it is an opinion, then you can write a paragraph about it.

Work with a partner and decide which sentence, A or B, is a fact.

1. **A**   Rice is a cereal.

   B   Different countries eat rice in their own different ways.

2. **A**   The potato is a vegetable.

   B   Potatoes are good for you.

3. **A**   Rice contains starch.

   B   Rice can be cooked in different ways.

4. **A**   Drinking too much coffee is bad for your health.

   B   Coffee is made from coffee beans.

5. **A**   Chewing gum is good for you.

   B   Chewing gum is made from plastic and rubber.

6. **A**   Coffee contains caffeine.

   B   Different countries have their own ways of making coffee.

Another kind of *topic sentence* gives the topic different parts.

Example:

A. Potatoes are good for you in three ways.

B. There are four basic methods of eating french fries.

C. Potato-eaters fall into three groups.

A, B, and C are topic sentences. They are not facts. Look at sentence A. Someone may disagree with you and say that potatoes are good for you in *four* ways. When you use this kind of topic sentence you need to support your opinion. For example, you need to write about three ways potatoes are good for you.

Exercise 4

Put a checkmark (✔) in the blank if the sentence is a topic sentence.

_____ 1. Bread is made from flour.

_____ 2. Drinking too much coffee may be dangerous for you in several ways.

_____ 3. In some countries people have very different ideas about drinking tea.

_____ 4. Potatoes are a root vegetable.

_____ 5. Rice is the basic food for half of the world's population.

_____ 6. Potatoes contain many nutrients.

_____ 7. Rice may be cooked in four ways.

_____ 8. Rice is the staple food in many countries.

WRITING PRACTICE

Choose one of the topics below:
1. The basic food in my country
2. The main drink in my country

....

1. Pre-writing.

Work with a group, a partner, or alone.

1. Write down the topic at the top of your paper. (Say what your main food or drink is.)

2. Then, ask a question about your topic. This will help you to get ideas. Choose one of these questions words.

   Who?
   What?/In what way?
   Where?
   When?
   Why?

For example:

Rice is an important food in my country.

Question: Why?

3. Write down as many answers as you can. If you find the question word does not work, try another question word.

2. Develop an outline.

A. Organize your ideas.

Step 1: *Write a topic sentence.*

Step 2: *Choose some of the answers to your question as support sentences.*

B. **Make a more detailed outline. The paragraph outline below will help you.**

Paragraph **Outline**

_____ (Topic sentence) _____.
(Supporting fact) _____
_____. (Supporting fact) _____
_____.
(Supporting fact) _____
_____.
(Concluding sentence) _____.

3. Write a rough draft.

4. Revise your rough draft.

Using the checklist below, check your rough draft or let your partner check it.

Paragraph Checklist

_____ 1. Does your paragraph have a title?

_____ 2. Did you indent the first line?

_____ 3. Did you write on every other line of the paper? (Look at pages 6–7 for instructions on paragraph form.)

_____ 4. Does your paragraph have a topic sentence?

_____ 5. Does your topic sentence have a controlling idea?

_____ 6. Do your sentences support your topic sentence?

_____ 7. Are your ideas in the correct order?

_____ 8. Does your paragraph have a concluding sentence?

5. Edit your paragraph.

Work with a partner or a teacher to edit your paragraph. Correct spelling, punctuation, vocabulary, and grammar.

6. Write your final copy.

Chapter 4: Delicacies

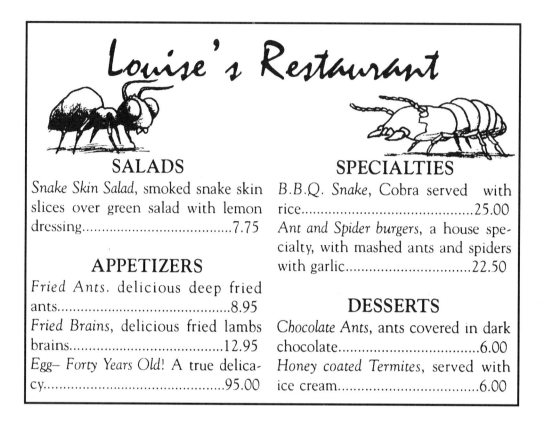

Louise's Restaurant

SALADS

Snake Skin Salad, smoked snake skin slices over green salad with lemon dressing..7.75

APPETIZERS

Fried Ants. delicious deep fried ants..8.95
Fried Brains, delicious fried lambs brains..12.95
Egg– Forty Years Old! A true delicacy..95.00

SPECIALTIES

B.B.Q. Snake, Cobra served with rice..25.00
Ant and Spider burgers, a house specialty, with mashed ants and spiders with garlic..22.50

DESSERTS

Chocolate Ants, ants covered in dark chocolate..6.00
Honey coated Termites, served with ice cream..6.00

PRE-READING QUESTIONS

Discuss these questions with your classmates or teacher.

1. Discuss the items on the menu.
2. Which ones do you want to eat?
3. Which ones do you not want to eat? Say why.

Reading: Delicacies

Would you like some chicken's feet? How about frog's legs? Well, you can't say no to a fifty-year-old egg! It's a **delicacy** that people pay a lot of money for, believe it or not. People all over the world eat just about everything from elephant's trunks to monkey's brains.

Snakes and eels are delicacies in most parts of the world. In France and England, fish shops sell eels that are **alive**. In Asia, there are special restaurants for snakes. Everything on the menu is snake: snake soup, snake **appetizers**, snake main course, and snake **desserts**! When you go to the restaurant the snakes are alive. You choose the snakes you want to eat. Then the waiter kills the snakes before your very eyes!

Insects like termites, ants, and bees are delicacies to many people. In Africa, people fight over termite nests. They eat the termites alive and say they taste like pineapple. In India, people make the ants into a **paste** and eat them with curry. In Borneo, people mix the ants with rice. They say it gives the rice a special **flavor**. In Australia, the **native** people drink ants. They **mash** them in water and say the drink tastes like lemonade! And bees are delicious when you fry them. You just can't stop eating them!

VOCABULARY

Rewrite each sentence, replacing the underlined words with one of the words below.

delicacy	appetizers	paste	flavor
mash	alive	desserts	native

1. Each country has its <u>special dish.</u>

   _____

   _____

2. In some countries, shops sell fish, eels, and snakes that are <u>not dead.</u>

   _____

   _____

3. People in Borneo make ants into a <u>soft, smooth cream.</u>

_____

_____

4. Some insects have a special <u>taste.</u>

_____

_____

5. People in Australia <u>crush</u> ants in water and then drink them.

_____

_____

6. In Asia, there are restaurants where the <u>small, delicious things you</u> <u>eat at the beginning of a meal</u> are snake.

_____

_____

7. The <u>original</u> people of Australia like ants, too.

_____

_____

8. You can even have snake <u>sweet food that you eat at the end of</u> <u>a meal.</u>

_____

_____

A. Looking for the Main Ideas

Circle the letter of the best answer.

1. All over the world people eat _____.

    a. only frog's legs

    b. just about everything

    c. only legs, brains, and eggs

2. In most parts of the world snakes and eels are _____.

    a. delicacies

    b. only appetizers

    c. not found in fish shops or restaurants

3. Insects are _____.

    a. only good with lemonade

    b. special in pineapple

    c. delicious to many people

B. Looking for Details

Circle T if the sentence is true. Circle F if the sentence is false.

1. In Asia, there are special restaurants for snakes.	T	F
2. In Australia, they mash ants in rice.	T	F
3. In India, people make ants into a soup.	T	F
4. Bees are delicious when you fry them.	T	F
5. In Africa, people say ants taste like eels.	T	F
6. Some people pay a lot of money for old eggs.	T	F

Discuss these questions with your classmates.

1. Do you know about other strange food that people eat?

2. Did you ever eat a food that was different for you? What was it like?

3. Describe a delicacy that people eat in your country.

Now read the following paragraph written by a student. Can you guess where the student is from?

Model Paragraph

A Specialty in My Country

The people in my country, X, make a special dish from the izote flower which is delicious to eat. The flower grows on top of a beautiful tree. You can see these trees in gardens of houses. You can also buy izote flowers in the market. The best time for the flower is in the summer, from November to March. From the flowers we make a special dish that we eat almost every week in the summer. To prepare this dish, we boil the petals of the flower in water with salt and garlic. Then we take out the petals and add them to beaten eggs. We fry this mixture like an omelet. When it is ready, we eat it with tomato sauce. The izote flower is a special flower in my country, X.

ORGANIZING

Topic Sentence
Support
Support
Support
Support
Support
Concluding Sentence

Supporting Sentences

Supporting sentences tell you more about the topic sentence. Supporting sentences give the reader more facts about or examples of the topic sentence.

Example:

> **Topic sentence:** The people in my country make a special dish from the izote flower.
>
> **Supporting sentences:** where the flower grows
> where you can buy the flower
> when you can buy the flower
> when you eat the dish
> how you make it
> how you eat it

Exercise 1

Look at the following groups of sentences. The topic sentence is underlined. All the sentences in each group support the topic sentence except for one. Find the sentence that does not support the topic sentence. Circle the letter of your answer.

1. The carambola is a popular fruit in Taiwan.
   a. It is not expensive.
   b. You can buy it in any supermarket or fruit store in my country.
   c. It is good for you when you are sick.
   d. Most Americans do not like the carambola.

2. The platano, which looks like a banana, has many uses in my country, Peru.
   a. It is an export for my country.
   b. It is used in many kinds of dishes.
   c. Bananas are also a favorite.
   d. It is a supplement for milk.

3. Ginger is a traditional seasoning in China.
   a. It is used in many traditional dishes.
   b. The Chinese have used ginger for a long time.
   c. It is an old custom to use ginger when the dish has a strong smell.
   d. Ginger is expensive in the United States.

4. Soya beans are becoming popular all over the world.

      a. They have always been popular in Asia.

      b. They are easy to grow.

      c. They are not as good as meat.

      d. They have a high food value.

The Concluding Sentence

The last sentence in your paragraph is called the **concluding sentence**. This sentence tells the reader it is the end of the paragraph.

The concluding sentence and the topic sentence are similar. They are both general sentences. You can write the concluding sentence like the topic sentence, but use different words.

There are two ways to write a **concluding sentence**:

1. Say the topic sentence in *different* words.

or

2. Summarize the main points in the paragraph.

Begin a **concluding sentence** with one of these phrases:

    In conclusion, . . .

or

    In summary, . . .

Exercise 2

Write a concluding sentence for each of the topic sentences below.

Example:

    Topic sentence: Kimchi is an indispensable side dish at meals in
                           Korea.

    Concluding sentence: In conclusion, there is no day without kimchi
                               on the table in my country, Korea.

1. In Japan, we use seaweed in many of our traditional meals.

    _____

    _____

2. Americans eat turkey on two of their traditional holidays.

    _____

    _____

3. In many countries, it is usual to eat food with hot peppers.

_____

_____

4. Beans play an important part in Brazilian food.

_____

_____

5. The French like to eat cheese and have over three hundred

different cheeses.

_____

_____

WRITING PRACTICE

1. Pre-writing.

Work with a group, a partner, or alone.
1. Write the name of the specialty or delicacy in your country (the topic).
2. Now write a controlling idea about the topic. (Say why it is important/special/traditional.)
3. Then ask questions about your controlling idea. Use some of the following question words: When? Where? Who? How? Why?

Example:
A traditional food in my country is bean sprout soup.

When do you eat it?
How do you make it?
Why do people eat it?
etc.

2. Develop an outline.

A. Organize your ideas.

Step 1: *Write a topic sentence.*

Step 2: *Choose some of the answers to your questions to use as support sentences.*

B. Make a more detailed outline. The paragraph outline below will help you.

Paragraph Outline

   (Topic sentence)   .
(Supporting sentence 1)   .
(Supporting sentence 2)   .
(Supporting sentence 3)   .
(Supporting sentence 4)   .
(Concluding sentence)   .

3. Write a rough draft.

4. Revise your rough draft.

Using the checklist below, check your rough draft or let your partner check it.

Paragraph Checklist

_____ 1. Does your paragraph have a title?

_____ 2. Did you indent the first line?

_____ 3. Did you write on every other line of the paper?

_____ 4. Does your paragraph have a topic sentence?

_____ 5. Does your topic sentence have a controlling idea?

_____ 6. Do your sentences support your topic sentence?

_____ 7. Are your ideas in the correct order?

_____ 8. Does your paragraph have a concluding sentence?

5. Edit your paragraph.

Work with a partner or a teacher to edit your paragraph. Correct spelling, punctuation, vocabulary, and grammar.

6. Write your final copy.

Are these facts true or false? Circle your answer.

1. The Irish drink more tea than any other people.   T   F

2. American children eat more candy than any other nationality.   T   F

3. It is possible to eat a different kind of hamburger every day in the United States for a whole year.   T   F

4. America's favorite fruit is the apple.   T   F

5. The basic food of half of the world's population is rice.   T   F

6. Peanuts grow on small trees.   T   F

7. The ancient Romans ate mice.   T   F

8. Apple pie is America's favorite dessert.   T   F

9. One pound of spaghetti, if the pieces are put end to end, will measure 320 feet.   T   F

10. The average American chews twenty-four packs of chewing gum a year.   T   F

UNIT 3

Customs and Traditions

Chapter 5: How Do They Bathe?

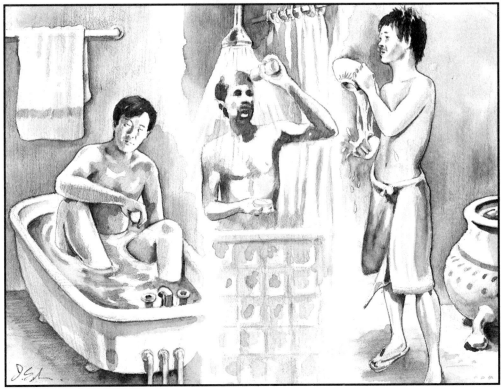

PRE-READING QUESTIONS

1. What are the people in the picture doing?

2. Why do people bathe?

3. What kinds of bathing do you know?

Reading: How Do They Bathe?

Everyone **bathes** in a different way. Most Americans never take a bath. They soap and **rinse off** under the shower. The English always take a bath. First, they sit in a **bathtub** full of warm water. Then they soap themselves, and finally, they rinse off the soap, all in the same water. The Japanese, on the other hand, first wash with soap in the shower. Then they go and sit in a bathtub full of warm water for twenty minutes or more. Later, others in the family use the same water to sit and relax in.

The Thai do not get into a shower or a bathtub. They stand in a room or **area** of a house where there is a big **jar** full of water. With a **bowl** they pour water from the jar on themselves. So that other people do not see their bodies, the Thai always wear a long piece of cloth called a pasin around their bodies. They wear this when they are bathing.

Everyone gets clean in a different way. We know that washing is good and **healthy** for us. But this was not true in the past. Up to 1800, most Americans did not bathe because they thought it was bad for them.

VOCABULARY

Rewrite each sentence, replacing the underlined words with one of the words or phrases below.

bathes	rinse off	bathtub	an area
bowl	healthy	jar	

1. Everyone <u>washes himself</u> in a different way.

   _____

   _____

2. The Thai have a <u>big container like a vase</u> full of water.

   _____

   _____

3. The English sit in a <u>large container where you sit to wash your</u>

   <u>whole body</u>.

   _____

   _____

4. Washing is <u>good for your body</u>.

_____

_____

5. The English <u>wash with water to take off the soap</u> in the same water they sit in.

_____

_____

6. The Thai wash in <u>a part</u> of the house where there is a big jar.

_____

_____

7. The Thai use a <u>small round container that holds liquid</u> to pour water on themselves.

_____

_____

COMPREHENSION

A. Looking for the Main Ideas

Circle the letter of the correct answer.

1. Everyone _____.

    a. takes a bath

    b. bathes in a different way

    c. takes a shower

2. The Thai _____.

    a. have a shower

    b. have a bath

    c. do not have a bath or a shower

3. People _____.

    a. have different ways to get clean

    b. think it is bad to get clean

    c. always bathed

B. Looking for Details

One word in each sentence is not correct. Rewrite the sentence with the correct word.

1. The Japanese first wash with soap in the bathtub.

   _____

   _____

2. The English always take a shower.

   _____

   _____

3. First, the English stand in a bathtub full of warm water.

   _____

   _____

4. Most Americans always take a bath.

   _____

   _____

5. The Thai pour water on themselves with a jar.

   _____

   _____

6. Up to 1800, most Americans did not relax.

   _____

   _____

DISCUSSION

Find out from the students in your class how they bathe in their country. Fill out the questionnaire below.

Name	Country	Kind of Bathing shower/bath/ shower and bath/public bath	How many times a week?
Dong	Korea	public bath	once

Discuss these questions with your classmates.

1. Which is better, a shower or a bath? Say why.
2. What do you know about a public bath?
3. Is it bad for your health if you do not bathe?

WRITING

Now read the following paragraph written by a student. Can you guess where the student is from?

Model Paragraph

Bathing in My Country

In my country, X, we take a special bath at home once a week. The bathroom is tiled, with a tub, a shower, and a toilet. First, we take a shower with soap. If we do not have a shower we pour hot water on us with a bowl from the tub. Next, we get into the bathtub filled with hot water. We stay in the bathtub for about fifteen minutes. Then we get out of the bathtub and rub our bodies with a special rough towel. Finally, we soap our bodies and rinse it off. This is a long process but it is only once a week.

Describing a Process

When you want to tell about how you do something, like take a bath or wash your car, you must list the main steps. Make sure that the steps are in the correct order. Then to make the order clear to the reader, use the following words that show time order:

> First, . . . (Second, . . . Third, . . .)
> Next, . . .
> Then . . .
> Finally/Lastly, . . .

These words come at the beginning of a sentence. You use a comma (,) after each word except for **then**. You do not need to use these words for each sentence of your paragraph.

Now underline the words that show time order in the model paragraph.

Exercise 1

Put the following sentences in the correct order. Number them 1, 2, 3, 4, . . .

1. To wash your hair follow these steps.

    _____ Put some shampoo on your hair.

    _*1*_ Wet your hair with water.

    _____ Rinse off shampoo.

    _____ Lather your hair with shampoo.

    _____ Dry your hair with a towel.

    _____ Repeat the process.

2. Washing dishes is easy.

    _____ Wash plates in soapy water with a brush.

    _____ Remove pieces of food from plates.

    _____ Dry plates with a towel.

    _____ Rinse off soapy water.

3. Cleaning windows is not difficult.

_____ You need a bucket and a large sponge.

_____ Dry the windows with a paper towel.

_____ Wet the sponge and wipe the windows with it.

_____ Fill the bucket with water and a little ammonia.

_____ Your windows will shine.

PUNCTUATION

Comma(,) with Items in a Series

You use a comma to separate items in a series. Do not use a comma if there are only two items.

Examples:

The bathroom is tiled, with a tub, a shower, and a toilet.

A bathroom can have a shower, a tub, or both.

The bathroom has a shower and a toilet.
(No comma needed)

You can take a shower or a bath.
(No comma needed)

Exercise 2

Put commas in these sentences where necessary. Note that some sentences do not need a comma.

1. He went to the bathroom with a bar of soap shampoo some towels and a plastic bowl.

2. That week many people used the bathtub including his sister younger brother and grandfather.

3. You can take a hot or a cold bath.

4. In my country the bathroom has a shower and a bathtub.

5. People wash in different ways. They can pour water over their bodies or take a shower or sit in a bathtub.

6. You can take a shower or take a bath or go to the public bath.

WRITING PRACTICE

Choose one of the topics below:

1. Bathing in my country (at home)
2. Going to a public bath
3. Bathing a baby

1. Pre-writing.

Work with a partner. Tell your partner how you bathe. Then write down what you do first, then what you do next, and what you do after that . . .

2. Develop an outline.

Number your sentences in the correct order. Then rewrite all the sentences in a paragraph. Use the words showing time order. The paragraph outline below will help you.

Paragraph Outline

(Topic sentence)_____.
First,_____.
Next,_____.
Then_____.
Finally,_____.

(Do not begin every sentence with a word showing time order.)

3. Write a rough draft.

4. Revise your rough draft.

Using the checklist below, check your rough draft or let your partner check it.

Paragraph Checklist

_____ 1. Does your paragraph have a title?

_____ 2. Did you indent the first line?

_____ 3. Did you write on every other line of your paper? (Look at pages 6–7 for instructions on paragraph form.)

_____ 4. Does your paragraph have a topic sentence?

_____ 5. Are your ideas in the correct order?

_____ 6. Does your paragraph have a concluding sentence?

5. Edit your paragraph.

Work with a partner or your teacher to edit your paragraph. Correct spelling, punctuation, vocabulary, and grammar.

6. Write your final copy.

Chapter 6: Unusual Marriage Ceremonies

PRE-READING QUESTIONS

Discuss these questions with your classmates or teacher.

1 What are the people in the picture wearing?

2 What are they doing?

3 Why do you think people do these things?

Reading: Unusual Marriage Ceremonies

Marriage **ceremonies** around the world are very different. Some are short and simple; others are long and **complicated**. In some cases the bride wears red clothes, in others she may be tattooed. In the islands of New Guinea, north of Australia, girls who want to be beautiful brides are tattooed from head to foot. This takes several years. First, the hands are tattooed, and finally, the face. The marriage ceremony in New Guinea is unusual, too.

The wedding ceremony takes place in a room in the **bride**'s house. First, the bride and **bridegroom** stand back to back in the middle of the room. The guests and friends stand around them, the men on one side and the women on the other. Next, an old man joins their right hands together. He **spits** a mouthful of water over them. He says, "May no enemy kill you; may no bad spirit bring you sickness." After that, somebody brings some sago, a kind of thick, white soup. After the new husband and wife eat some, the guests have some. Then the **newlyweds** sit up for four nights. During this time their friends watch them and do not let them fall asleep. They do this to have a long and rich life. Finally, everybody leaves them to meet alone on the night of the fifth day.

VOCABULARY

What is the meaning of the underlined words? Circle the letter of the correct answer.

1. Marriage <u>ceremonies</u> around the world are different.
    a. customs you follow on a special occasion
    b. the clothes you wear on a special occasion

2. In some cases the wedding ceremony is long and <u>complicated</u>.
    a. unhappy
    b. not simple

3. The ceremony takes place in the house of the <u>bride</u>.
    a. the woman who is going to be married
    b. the man who is going to be married

4. The bride and the bridegroom stand back to back.

    a. the father of the girl to be married

    b. the man who is going to be married

5. An old man spits a mouthful of water.

    a. drinks slowly

    b. forces the liquid out of his mouth

6. The newlyweds sit up for four nights.

    a. the new husband and wife

    b. the guests at the wedding

COMPREHENSION

A. Looking for the Main Ideas

Circle the letter of the correct answer.

1. Marriage ceremonies around the world are _____.

    a. short

    b. long

    c. different

2. The marriage ceremony in New Guinea _____.

    a. is simple

    b. is unusual

    c. takes several years

3. The newlyweds in New Guinea must _____.

    a. not sleep for four nights

    b. sleep for four nights

    c. eat only at night

B. Looking for Details

Circle T if the sentence is true. Circle F if the sentence is false.

1. The wedding takes place in the bridegroom's house.	T	F
2. The bride and bridegroom stand in the back of the room.	T	F
3. An old man spits water over them.	T	F
4. The husband and wife eat some sago.	T	F
5. The guests at the ceremony do not eat sago.	T	F
6. The newlyweds meet alone on the fourth day.	T	F

Discuss these questions with your classmates.

1. What do the bride and the bridegroom wear in your country?
2. Who pays for the wedding in your country?
3. Describe the wedding ceremony in your country.

WRITING

Now read the following paragraph written by a student. What country does the student come from?

Model Paragraph

A Wedding in My Country

Last year my oldest brother got married. His bride was his friend's sister. First, they had a civil marriage in the town hall. A few weeks later, they had a church wedding. The bride wore a beautiful white dress with a veil over her face. The bridegroom wore a tuxedo. After the religious ceremony was over, the newlyweds and the guests went to a restaurant near the church. Here there was a wonderful wedding reception with all kinds of hot and cold food. After that, there was music and dancing. Before the reception ended, the bride and groom met and thanked every guest. Finally, after the reception was over, the newlyweds went on a trip to Hawaii for their honeymoon.

Review of Describing a Process

We know the words below show time order (Chapter 5):

First, . . .

Next, . . .

Then. . .

Finally/Lastly, . . .

The words **after that** also shows time order. We use these words in the same way as **next** and **then**.

After that, Next, Then	there was music and dancing.

We use **after that**, **next**, and **then** at the beginning of a sentence. We cannot use them to make two sentences into a single sentence.

Using *Before* and *After* to Show Time Order

When we describe a process, we often use dependent clauses beginning with **before** or **after**. These words show us time order.

A **clause** is a group of words with a subject and a verb. There are two kinds of clauses: main clauses and dependent clauses. A main clause is a separate sentence. A dependent clause depends on the main clause. It cannot stand alone.

Exercise 1

Read each of the following clauses. If the clause is a separate sentence and can stand alone, write "main clause" under it. If the clause cannot stand alone, write "dependent clause" under it.

1. they stand in the middle of the room

   main clause

2. before we eat

_____

3. after they finish the ceremony

_____

4. the newlyweds go on a trip for their honeymoon

_____

5. before the marriage ceremony begins

_____

6. the newlyweds sit up for four nights

_____

7. the bride wears a beautiful white dress

_____

8. after the newlyweds eat

_____

Writing a Dependent Clause with *Before* and *After*

Look at the sentences below. Each sentence has a main clause and a dependent clause.

After the religious ceremony is over, they go to a restaurant.
        Dependent clause

Before the reception ends, they thank every guest.
        Dependent clause

When the dependent clauses come first, you separate it from the main clause by a comma.

Punctuate the following sentences with a comma where necessary.

1. Before the dinner ended they thanked their friends.
2. After they had the food there was music.
3. Before they had the church wedding they had a civil marriage.
4. After the reception was over the newlyweds went on a honeymoon.
5. Before they had the reception they had a church wedding.
6. After they had their honeymoon they started a new life together.

Combine each pair of sentences into a single sentence with the words in parentheses. Begin with your dependent clause.

1. You have a religious ceremony.

   You have a wedding reception. (after)

   After you have a religious ceremony, you have a wedding reception.

2. We have a civil marriage.

   We have a church wedding. (before)

   _____

   _____

3. In New Guinea, the newlyweds eat some sago. (after)

   The guests eat some sago.

   _____

   _____

4. The wedding reception finishes. (after)

   The newlyweds go on a trip.

   _____

   _____

Choose **one** *of the topics below:*

1. A wedding reception in my country
2. A religious wedding ceremony in my country
3. Getting ready for a wedding in my country

1. Pre-writing.

Work with a partner. Tell your partner about a wedding in your country. Then write down what they do first, then what comes next, and after that . . .

2. Develop an outline.

Number your sentences in the correct order. Then rewrite all the sentences in a paragraph. Use the words showing time order. The paragraph outline below will help you.

Paragraph Outline

    (Topic sentence) _____.
First, _____.
Next, _____.
After that/Then _____.
After/Before _____.
Finally, _____.

3. Write a rough draft.

4. Revise your rough draft.

Using the checklist below, check your rough draft or let your partner check it.

Paragraph Checklist

_____ 1. Does your paragraph have a title?

_____ 2. Did you indent the first line?

_____ 3. Did you write on every other line?

_____ 4. Does your paragraph have a topic sentence?

_____ 5. Are your ideas in the correct order?

_____ 6. Does your paragraph have a concluding sentence?

5. Edit your paragraph.

Work with a partner or your teacher to edit your paragraph. Correct spelling, punctuation, vocabulary, and grammar.

6. Write your final copy.

DO YOU KNOW THESE AMERICAN CUSTOMS AND TRADITIONS?

Circle T if the answer is the true. Circle F if the answer is false.

1. At the end of a letter or note an "X" sign means a kiss.   T   F
2. In the United States you cannot hear the national anthem   T   F
   or song at sports games.
3. A potluck party is a party where you can play a game and   T   F
   win some money.
4. It is the custom in the United States to use a toothpick   T   F
   after a meal in front of other people.
5. A bride in her wedding dress in the United States must also   T   F
   have something old, something new, something borrowed,
   and something blue.
6. A leap year is one year in four when the month of February   T   F
   has 29 days. It is the custom that a woman can ask a man
   to marry her in a leap year.
7. In the United States it is the custom to eat with one hand   T   F
   and keep the hand that you do not use on your lap.
8. In the United States it is the custom to snap your fingers to   T   F
   get attention.

UNIT 4

Famous
People

Chapter 7: Louis Braille

PRE-READING QUESTIONS

Discuss these questions with your classmates or teacher.

1. What are the hands in the picture doing?
2. How can blind people read?
3. What do you know about blind people?

Reading: Louis Braille

Louis Braille was born near Paris, France. He was a very **smart** child. He liked to play with his father's work **tools**. One day, when he was four, a **sharp** tool went into his left eye. An **infection** started and went to both eyes. He was **unlucky**. A few weeks later, Louis was **blind.**

At age ten, Louis went to a school for blind children in Paris. One day a French soldier, Charles Barbier, visited the school. Barbier **invented** a system of night-reading. This system used **dots** for the letters of the alphabet. Soldiers used this system in time of war. Barbier thought this system could help blind people to read.

Barbier's system was difficult, but it gave Louis an idea. He made Barbier's system easier. By age fifteen, his new system was ready! Now he wanted blind schools to use his system. He was unlucky again. The schools did not want his system. Louis died in 1852 at age forty-three. Two years after he died, the blind schools began to use his system.

Today we call this system Braille after Louis Braille. His system is used for all languages, and for math, science, writing music, and computers for the blind.

VOCABULARY

Complete the sentences. Circle the letter of the correct answer.

1. Louis was a _____ child.

   a. night

   b. smart

2. When Louis was a child, he played with his father's _____.

   a. tools

   b. languages

3. A _____ tool went into his eye.

   a. left

   b. sharp

4. Louis got _____ in his eye.

    a. a system

    b. an infection

5. Louis became _____ when he was four years old.

    a. blind

    b. French

6. Charles Barbier _____ a system of night-reading.

    a. visited

    b. invented

7. Barbier's system used _____.

    a. tools

    b. dots

8. Louis was _____ again in life.

    a. blind

    b. unlucky

COMPREHENSION

A. Looking for the Main Ideas

Circle the letter of the best answer.

1. When Louis was four, he _____.

    a. became blind

    b. had sharp tools

    c. went to school

2. Charles Barbier _____.

    a. had an infection

    b. invented a system of night-reading

    c. visited soldiers

3. By age fifteen Louis _____.

    a. died

    b. was difficult

    c. made a new system of reading

B. Looking for Details

One word in each sentence is not correct. Rewrite the sentence with the correct word.

1. When Louis was four, a blind tool went into his eye.

2. Louis went to a school for unlucky children in Paris.

3. Soldiers used Barbier's system in time of math.

4. Barbier's system used tools for the letters of the alphabet.

5. Barbier thought his system could help blind people to play.

6. Louis died at age thirty-four.

Discuss these questions with your classmates.

1. Do you know of other famous blind people? How are blind people special?

2. Louis Braille was unlucky. Do you know another unlucky person? Explain.

WRITING

Now read the following paragraph written by a student.

Model Paragraph

My Sister Liz

My sister Liz was born lucky. She has a beautiful smile. When she does something bad, she smiles and my parents are not angry. She eats a lot and does not get fat. Her favorite meal is a double cheeseburger with french fries, a milkshake, and an ice cream sundae. She does not study hard but always gets good grades. After school she does her homework in five minutes while she watches television at the same time. In conclusion, I believe some people are born lucky, some are not.

ORGANIZING

Unity

As we know, a good paragraph must have three parts: a topic sentence, supporting sentences, and a concluding sentence. But a good paragraph must also have **unity**.

Unity means that all of the supporting sentences must be about the controlling idea in the topic sentence. Think about the model paragraph above.

Topic sentence: My sister Liz was <u>born lucky</u>.

(Controlling idea)

Main supporting sentences:

1. She has a beautiful smile.
2. She eats a lot and does not get fat.
3. She does not study hard but get good grades.

This paragraph has **unity**. All the supporting sentences are about why she was born lucky.

Irrelevant Sentences

When a sentence does not belong in a paragraph, we say it is an **irrelevant sentence**.

Example:

My sister Jamie is very shy. When there are other people around, she speaks very little. Sometimes she does not speak at all, and even runs away. She is very quiet at home and at school. You do not even know she is there sometimes. She is shy about her body, too. She never goes to the beach or swimming pool. But she likes ice cream and cookies.

Irrelevant sentence: But she likes ice cream and cookies.

This sentence does not talk about why she is shy. This sentence does not belong in the paragraph.

Exercise 1

Underline the irrelevant sentences in the following short paragraphs.

1. George has not been lucky in school this year. He got sick and missed classes, and could not take his finals. He also lost his books. These were not only textbooks but also his notebooks. Everybody likes George because he will go out of his way to help people.

2. My roommate Tony is very untidy. He has brown hair and blue eyes. He always leaves his laundry on the floor. When he cooks, he never washes the dishes. For a while, he had a bicycle on his bed. It is not surprising that Tony can never find anything.

3. My Uncle Conrad is very clumsy. When he drinks coffee he always spills some on his shirt. In the shopping mall he walks into other people all the time. He has size 14 feet. Last time he came to our house he sat on the cat.

4. Aunt Dotty loves adventure. On her sixtieth birthday she went mountain climbing in the Alps. On her seventieth birthday she went on a trip to the North Pole. When she was eighty, she drove, alone, across the United States. She loves to eat chocolate. We all wonder what she will do when she is ninety.

WRITING PRACTICE

Choose one of the topics below:
1. Describe a person who is lucky or unlucky.
2. Describe a good or bad quality of a friend or family member.
3. Describe a pet cat or dog.

1. Pre-writing.

Work with a partner or alone.

1. Write down a topic sentence about a person or animal. You can follow this outline for a topic sentence:

   What person/animal is to you + name + adjective

   My pet dog   Rex   is   very lazy

2. List as many points as you can about the person/animal.

3. Go over each point on your list. Ask yourself, "Does this support the controlling idea?" Cross out the points that do not.

2. Develop an outline.

A. Organize your ideas.

List the points in the order you will write about them in your paragraph.

B. Make a more detailed outline. The paragraph outline below will help you.

Paragraph Outline

(Topic sentence) _____.
(Supporting sentence 1) _____.
(Supporting detail(s)) _____.
(Supporting sentence 2) _____.
(Supporting detail(s)) _____.
(Supporting sentence 3) _____.
(Supporting detail(s)) _____.
(Concluding sentence) _____.

3. Write a rough draft.

4. Revise your rough draft.

Using the checklist below, check your rough draft or let your partner check it.

Paragraph Checklist

_____ 1. Does your paragraph have a title?

_____ 2. Did you indent the first line?

_____ 3. Did you write on every other line of your paper?

_____ 4. Does your paragraph have a topic sentence?

_____ 5. Does your topic sentence have a controlling idea?

_____ 6. Do your sentences support your topic sentence?

_____ 7. Are your ideas in the correct order?

_____ 8. Does your paragraph have a concluding sentence?

5. Edit your paragraph.

Work with a partner or your teacher to edit your paragraph. Correct spelling, punctuation, vocabulary, and grammar.

6. Write your final copy.

Chapter 8: The World's Most Unusual Millionaire

PRE-READING QUESTIONS

Discuss these questions with your classmates or teacher.

1. Describe the woman in the picture.
2. Do you think she looks like a millionaire? Why not?
3. What do you expect a millionaire to look like?

Reading: The World's Most Unusual Millionaire

Hetty Robinson was born in 1834. When her parents died, they left her $10 million. She was very good at business and made more money. Soon Hetty became the richest woman in the United States, but she was very **stingy**.

Hetty always wore the same black dress. The color of the dress changed to green and then to brown as the years passed by. Her undergarments were old newspapers she got from **trash** baskets. Her home was a **run-down** apartment with no heat in New Jersey. All she ate was onions, eggs, and cold oatmeal. She was too stingy to heat her food.

She was married for a short time to a millionaire, Edward Green, and had a son. She was even stingy with her own child. For example, when her son hurt his knee in an accident, Hetty did not call a doctor. She dressed her son in old clothes and took him to a free clinic. The doctors **recognized** her and asked for money. Hetty **refused** and took her son home. The boy did not get **medical treatment**, and a few years later his leg was amputated. When Hetty Green died in 1916, she left more than $100 million!

VOCABULARY

Complete the sentences with one of the following words.

stingy	run-down	trash
medical treatment	refused	recognized

1. When a person does not like to spend money, he or she is

   _____.

2. When people do not take care of an old apartment, it is

   _____.

3. People throw old newspapers they do not need in

   _____ baskets.

4. When the doctors saw Hetty and knew who she was, they

   _____ her.

5. When the doctors asked Hetty for money, she

_____ and did not give

them any.

6. The boy hurt his knee but did not see a doctor. He did not get

_____.

COMPREHENSION

A. Looking for the Main Ideas

Circle the letter of the best answer.

1. Hetty was a very rich woman, but she was _____.

    a. stingy

    b. short

    c. green

2. Hetty wore _____.

    a. cold undergarments

    b. three dresses

    c. the same black dress

3. Hetty was even stingy with _____.

    a. Edward Green

    b. her own child

    c. her leg

B. Looking for Details

Circle T if the sentence is true. Circle F if the sentence is false.

1. Hetty was the richest woman in the world.	T	F
2. Hetty only ate eggs, onions, and cold oatmeal.	T	F
3. Hetty called a doctor for her son.	T	F
4. Hetty got her undergarments from trash baskets.	T	F
5. Hetty lived in an apartment with no heat.	T	F
6. When Hetty died she left $10 million.	T	F

Discuss these questions with your classmates.

1. What famous person in the world do you know who had a bad character? Say what he/she did.
2. Tell us about a person you know who is stingy.
3. Describe some other types of people who are not very nice, and say why.

WRITING

Now read the following paragraph written by a student.

Model Paragraph

My Selfish Brother

My brother is very selfish. He does not want to share things with other people. For example, when he buys a bar of chocolate, he puts it in a secret place. Then he eats it all, by himself. He never helps anyone. He says he is busy. For example, a game of tennis or Nintendo makes him very busy. He does not care if something he does bothers other people. For instance, last night he played loud rock 'n roll music until four o'clock in the morning. In conclusion, I think my brother is selfish, and will always be selfish.

ORGANIZING

Giving Examples

To introduce an example in your paragraph, you can use the following:

or

For example↓, . . .
For instance↓, . . .

Now underline the words showing examples in the model paragraph. Next, look at the use of the comma with the words showing examples. Now go back and circle all the commas with the words showing examples.

In the model paragraph we use **for example** or **for instance** to give details about supporting sentences:

> **Topic sentence:** My brother is very selfish.
> **Supporting sentence:** He does not share things with other people.
> **Detail or example of supporting sentence:** For example, when he buys a bar of chocolate, he puts it in a secret place.

For example and **for instance** have the same meaning. When your sentence begins with **for example** or **for instance**, put a comma after these words.

> **For example**↓, when he buys a bar of chocolate, he puts it in a secret place.

or

> **For instance**↓, when he buys a bar of chocolate, he puts it in a secret place.

A sentence that begins with **for example** or **for instance** must be a complete sentence.

> For example, Hetty Green. **(Not correct)**

> For example, Hetty Green was a millionaire. **(Correct)**

Exercise 1

The following sentences are not complete or have mistakes. Write out correct sentences.

1. For example he gets food all over his shirt.

   _____

   _____

2. For instance, washes dishes.

   _____

   _____

3. For example: she never writes down my telephone messages.

   _____

   _____

4. For instance, a doctor.

_____

_____

5. For instance—she always leaves the bathroom in a mess.

_____

_____

A name of a person or a thing can follow an example.

More women are becoming leaders. **For example**, Margaret Thatcher and Golda Meir were both prime ministers of their countries.

Exercise 2

Work alone, with a partner, or in a group. Think of examples for the following statements. Add more if you can.

1. There have been many famous millionaires during this century.

   For example,_____,

   _____, and

   _____ are all millionaires.

2. There were some famous people who were very stingy. **For**

   instance, _____,

   _____, and

   _____ were all stingy.

3. Some people in history were very bad. **For example,**

   _____,

   _____,

   and _____ all did

   terrible things.

Write a complete sentence as an example for each statement. Use **for instance** *or* **for example** *in the correct form.*

1. My grandfather is very forgetful.

   _____

   _____

2. My English teacher has an excellent memory.

   _____

   _____

3. My sister is not an electrician, but she can fix many electrical

   things in the house.

   _____

   _____

WRITING PRACTICE

Choose **one** *of the topics below:*
   1. A stingy person you know
   2. A person who has had a bad character (selfish, inconsiderate, lazy, etc.)
   3. An unusual person

1. Pre-writing.

Work with a partner or alone.

1. Write down a topic sentence about a person. (Choose from the topics above.)
2. List as many points as you can about the person.
3. Go over each point on your list. Ask yourself, "Does this support the controlling idea?" Cross out the points that do not.
4. Think of an example for each point. If you cannot find an example, cross out the point.

2. Develop an outline.

Organize your ideas.

    A. List the points in the order you will write about them. You should have two or three points.

    B. Make a more detailed outline. The paragraph outline below will help you.

Paragraph `Outline`

(Topic sentence) _____.
(Supporting sentence 1) _____.
For example, _____.
(Supporting sentence 2) _____.
For instance, _____.
(Supporting sentence 3) _____.
_____, for example, _____.
(Concluding sentence) _____.

3. Write a rough draft.

4. Revise your rough draft.

Using the checklist below, check your rough draft or let your partner check it.

Paragraph Checklist

_____ 1. Does your paragraph have a title?

_____ 2. Did you indent the first line?

_____ 3. Did you write on every other line of the paper?

_____ 4. Does your paragraph have a topic sentence?

_____ 5. Does your topic sentence have a controlling idea?

_____ 6. Do your sentences support your topic sentence?

_____ 7. Are your ideas in the correct order?

_____ 8. Do you have examples?

_____ 9. Does your paragraph have a concluding sentence?

5. Edit your paragraph.

Work with a partner or your teacher to edit your paragraph. Correct spelling, punctuation, vocabulary, and grammar.

6. Write your final copy.

WHO ARE THEY?

1.  This president never smiled in any of his pictures. **Who was he?**

2.  This man made more than one thousand inventions. **Who was he?**

3.  This composer died a poor man at age thirty-five. **Who was he?**

4.  This African-American leader was killed in 1968. **Who was he?**

5.  This blind and deaf woman went to college and wrote books. **Who was she?**

6.  This nun went to India to look after the poor, sick, and dying. **Who is she?**

7.  This woman wrote the story of Frankenstein. **Who was she?**

UNIT 5

Nature's
Disasters

Chapter 9: The Earthquake of 1964

PRE-READING QUESTIONS

Discuss these questions with your classmates or teacher.

1. What do you think happened in the picture?

2. What has happened to the store in the picture?

3. What is wrong with the main street?

4. If you lost your possessions, including your house, in an earthquake, would you rebuild in the same place? Why or why not?

5. What is the worst earthquake you know about?

Reading: The Earthquake of 1964

March 27, 1964, was a holiday in Alaska. Most people were at home, and everything was **peaceful**. Then it happened. Suddenly, there was a sound, like the sound of **thunder**. Next, people's houses began to shake. Buildings **cracked** and fell. In the town of Anchorage, the main street went up ten feet, holes opened in the earth, and buildings fell in. The **earthquake** that hit Alaska measured 8.3 on the Richter Scale.

In the Pacific Ocean the earthquake made a **tidal wave**. This wave traveled at two hundred miles an hour. Shortly after, at about 6 P.M., it hit the **coast** of Alaska. It took away with it a piece of land four thousand feet long and six hundred feet wide. It traveled down the West Coast, and across to Hawaii and Japan. People tried to escape, but it destroyed many towns.

The earthquake of 1964 killed 130 people. It was one of the strongest earthquakes in North America. **Scientists** do not know when the next earthquake will **happen**. They are difficult to **predict**, but you will know when it hits.

VOCABULARY

Circle the letter of the word which correctly completes the sentence.

1. On March 27, 1964, _____ hit Alaska.

    a. an earthquake

    b. a street

2. No one can _____ an earthquake.

    a. predict

    b. travel

3. People were at home on this holiday, and the town was

    _____.

    a. strong

    b. peaceful

4. The people heard a sound like _____.

    a. thunder

    b. feet

5. The walls of the buildings in Anchorage _____.

    a. measured

    b. cracked

6. The Alaska earthquake made a _____ that traveled across the Pacific Ocean.

    a. town

    b. tidal wave

7. The tidal wave hit the _____ of Alaska.

    a. sound

    b. coast

8. _____ cannot predict the next earthquake.

    a. Scientists

    b. Holidays

9. No one knows when the next earthquake will _____.

    a. travel

    b. happen

COMPREHENSION

A. Looking for the Main Ideas

Write complete answers to these questions.

1. When was the earthquake?

    _____

    _____

2. What did the earthquake make in the Pacific Ocean?

    _____

    _____

3. Where did the tidal wave go after it hit Alaska?

    _____

    _____

4. How strong was the earthquake?

    _____

    _____

B. Looking for Details

Circle T if the sentence is true. Circle F if the sentence is false.

1. Scientists can always predict earthquakes.   T F
2. The earthquake had a sound like thunder at first.   T F
3. The tidal wave hit Alaska at 5 P.M.   T F
4. The tidal wave traveled at twenty miles per hour.   T F
5. The Alaska earthquake killed 130 people.   T F
6. A measurement of 8.3 on the Richter Scale is not strong.   T F
7. The tidal wave traveled down the East Coast.   T F
8. In Anchorage, buildings went up sixty feet.   T F

DISCUSSION

Discuss these questions with your classmates.

1. How can you prepare yourself for an earthquake?
2. Almost every day there is a new disaster in the news. It could be a flu virus that kills people. What makes you most afraid?
3. The disasters that we are most likely to remember are those that happen closest to where we live. Can you remember a disaster (fire, plane crash, etc.) that happened near where you lived? Tell us about it.

WRITING

Now read the following paragraph written by a student.

Model Paragraph

A Terrifying Day

October 1, 1987, was a terrifying day for me. It was 7:30 on a Thursday morning in Mexico. I was alone because my parents were out of town. Suddenly, the room started to shake. Some dishes fell to the floor. I did not know what to do so I got under the table. A few minutes later, I came out and tried to turn on the television, but the electricity was off. After that, I tried the telephone, but it did not work. Shortly after, the neighbors came to see if I was all right. Finally, at about 9:00 A.M., the telephone rang. It was my mother from Mexico City. She was more frightened than I was.

A Narrative Paragraph

The paragraph you just read is a **narrative paragraph.** A narrative paragraph tells a story about something that happened. In a narrative paragraph you must use a good time order for your sentences. This means that the sentences must be in the order that the story happened.

Exercise 1

The following sentences are about a terrifying day but they are not in the correct order of time. Number them in the correct order.

_____ a. I got under the table.

_____ b. I came out and tried the telephone, but it did not work.

_____ c. Shortly after that, the neighbors came to see if I was all right.

_____ d. The room started to shake.

The next step is to use words that show time order to connect your sentences. These words show the order in which things happened in time.

Words showing time order:

> October 1, 1987, . . .
>
> At 5 P.M., . . .
>
> Suddenly, . . .
>
> A few minutes later, . . .
>
> After that, . . .
>
> Shortly after that, . . .
>
> Finally, . . .

Now underline the words showing time order in the model paragraph.

PUNCTUATION

The Comma (,) with Time and Place Expressions

Look at the words showing time order. Look at the use of the comma after words showing time order. Now go back to the model paragraph and circle all the commas after the words showing time order.

We also use the comma with dates and place names.

Dates

a. We use a comma to separate a date from a year:

    I came to the United States on March 4, 1990.

    They were married in July 26, 1987.

b. We use a comma after the year when a sentence continues:

    October 1, 1987, was the day of the earthquake.

    On March 27, 1964, a big earthquake hit Alaska.

Place Names

a. We use a comma to separate a city from a state or a city from a country:

    We were at home in Anchorage, Alaska.

    I come from Tokyo, Japan.

b. We use a comma after a state or country when the sentence continues:

    Crescent City, California, is on the coast.

Exercise 2

Put a comma where necessary in the following sentences.

1. The San Francisco earthquake hit on the morning of April 18 1906.
2. On November 4 1951 a tidal wave hit Hawaii.
3. A tidal wave hit Crescent City California.
4. The biggest earthquake recorded in North America was the earthquake of March 27 1964.
5. Suddenly people heard a noise like thunder.
6. An earthquake hit Armenia in December 1988.
7. In Yokohama Japan there were a lot of fires.

8. Valdez Alaska was ten feet higher after the earthquake.

9. A few minutes later buildings fell.

10. Shortly after a tidal wave hit Alaska.

WRITING PRACTICE

Choose one of the topics below:
1. A frightening day
2. A dangerous experience
3. A strange experience

1. Pre-writing.

Work with a partner. Tell your partner about it. Then write answers to the questions below.

1. When and where did the experience occur?

_____

_____

2. What happened?

_____

_____

3. What happened after that?

_____

_____

2. Develop an outline.

Write the sentences in the order that they happened. Then, use the words showing time order. *The paragraph outline below will help you.*

Paragraph Outline

(date) was a _____ day for me. I was _____ _____ because _____.
Suddenly, _____.
A few minutes later, _____. Shortly after that, _____. Finally, _____
_____.

3. Write a rough draft.

4. Revise your rough draft.

Using the checklist below, check your rough draft or let your partner check it.

Paragraph Checklist

_____ 1. Does your paragraph have a title?

_____ 2. Did you indent the first line?

_____ 3. Did you write on every other line of the paper? (Look at pages 6–7 for instructions on paragraph form.)

_____ 4. Does your paragraph have a topic sentence?

_____ 5. Does your topic sentence have a controlling idea?

_____ 6. Do your sentences support your topic sentence?

_____ 7. Are your ideas in the correct order?

_____ 8. Does your paragraph have a concluding sentence?

5. Edit your paragraph.

Work with a partner or your teacher to edit your paragraph. Correct spelling, punctuation, vocabulary, and grammar.

6. Write your final copy.

Chapter 10: Killer Bees

PRE-READING QUESTIONS

Discuss these questions with your classmates or teacher.

1 What is happening in the picture?

2 What can happen to the person in the picture?

Reading: Killer Bees

Killer bees started in Brazil in 1957. A scientist in Sao Paulo wanted bees to make more honey. So he put forty-six African bees with some Brazilian bees. The bees **bred** and made a new kind of bee. But the new bees were a mistake. They did not want to make more honey. They wanted to **attack**. Then, by accident, twenty-six African bees **escaped** and bred with the Brazilian bees outside.

Scientists could not control the problem. The bees **spread**. They went from Brazil to Venezuela. Then they went to Central America. Now they are in North America. They travel about 390 miles a year. Each group of bees, or **colony**, grows four times a year. This means one million new colonies every five years.

Why are people afraid of killer bees? People are afraid for two reasons. First, the bees **sting** many more times than a normal bee. Killer bees can sting sixty times a minute non-stop for two hours. Second, killer bees attack in groups. Four hundred bee stings can kill a person.

Already **several** hundred people are dead. Now killer bees are in Texas. In a few years they will spread all over the United States. People can do nothing but wait.

VOCABULARY

Match each word with its definition. There is one extra definition.

1. breed	a. run away
2. attack	b. cover a larger area
3. escape	c. prick with pain
4. spread	d. a group of bees
5. sting	e. a few
6. colony	f. produce young
7. several	g. be violent
	h. eat

A. Looking for the Main Ideas

Circle the best answer.

1. A scientist wanted bees _____.
    a. to go to Africa
    b. to make more honey
    c. to attack

2. Scientists _____.
    a. could not control the problem
    b. went to Brazil
    c. grew every year

3. People are afraid of killer bees because _____.
    a. they sting
    b. they sting more and attack in groups
    c. they attack and die

B. Looking for Details

Circle the letter of the best answer.

1. A scientist in Brazil put _____.
    a. forty-six Brazilian bees with six African bees
    b. some Brazilian bees with forty-six African bees

2. Twenty-six bees _____.
    a. escaped from the laboratory
    b. bred with African bees

3. The killer bees went _____.
    a. from Brazil to Venezuela
    b. from central America to Venezuela

4. Killer bees _____.
    a. can sting sixty times a minute
    b. can sting four hundred times a minute

5. Killer bees travel _____.

    a. four times a year.

    b. about 390 miles a year.

6. Each group of killer bees _____.

    a. grows every five years

    b. grows four times a year

DISCUSSION

Discuss these questions with your classmates.

1. Have you been stung by a bee? What happened?
2. What is a good thing to do when a bee stings you?
3. What insects do you have in your country? Are these insects a problem?
4. What other insects or animals are you afraid of?

WRITING

Now read the following paragraph written by a student.

Model Paragraph

Cockroaches

    Cockroaches have become a major problem in our building for several reasons. First, cockroaches or roaches carry germs and disease. Because roaches inhabit areas where there is food, we may get sick from the food we eat. Second, roaches eat everything. They not only eat food but glue, paint, clothes, wallpaper, and even plastic. There is a feeling of horror and disgust because everything in our home has been destroyed by roaches. They even live in and eat the television set. Finally, roaches are indestructible. Nothing can kill the roaches in our building. All the chemical powders and sprays we have tried on them are no good. They are always back. It is either them or us, so we have decided to move out.

Giving Reasons

In this lesson you will learn how to **give reasons** for a situation. Usually, there is more than one reason for a situation. It is important to look at all the reasons. When there are many reasons, there is usually one which is most important.

When you write your reasons, remember the following:

1. Think of or discuss all the reasons. There are probably more than one.

2. Support your reasons. Give examples.

3. State your most important last. This will make your paragraph more interesting. If you give your most important reason first, the reader may not feel it necessary to read the rest of your paragraph.

Transition for Giving Reasons: *Because*

Because answers the question "Why?" **Because** comes before the part that gives the reason. The reason can be before or after the statement.

Examples:

> **Statement:** We may get sick from the food we eat.
>
> **Reason:** Roaches inhabit areas where there is food.
>
> We may get sick from the food we eat **because** roaches inhabit areas where there is food.

or

> **Because** roaches inhabit areas where there is food, we may get sick from the food we eat.

Note: Use a comma after the reason if you start the sentence with **because.**

Join the sentences with **because.**
Write each sentence in two ways:

1. **because** in the middle
2. **because** in the beginning

1. There is a feeling of disgust. Everything in our home has been

   destroyed by roaches.

   _____

   _____

2. We are going to move out. The roaches are not moving out.

   _____

   _____

3. Nothing can kill roaches. Roaches are indestructible.

   _____

   _____

4. People are afraid of the killer bees. The bees can sting many more

   times than a normal bee.

   _____

   _____

5. The killer bees are spreading. Scientists cannot control them.

   _____

   _____

Writing Practice

***Choose** one of the topics below:*
1. An animal or insect I dislike
2. An animal or insect that is a problem
3. A disease that is a problem

1. Pre-writing.

Work with a partner, a group, or alone.

1. Write down the topic at the top of your paper.
2. Then think of as many reasons about the topic as you can. Write every word or phrase that comes into your mind about the topic. Write down as much information as you can.
3. Write your ideas in any order you like. Do not worry if the idea is important or not. Write it down.

2. Develop an outline.

A. The next step is to organize your ideas.

Step 1: *Write the main idea sentence.*

Step 2: *Pick the best reasons from the ones you wrote.*

Step 3: *Order your reasons. Don't forget to put your most important reason last.*

Step 4: *Remember to use these transitions for giving reasons:*

The first reason is . . .	or	First, . . .
The second reason is . . .	or	Second, . . .
The final reason is . . .	or	Finally, . . .

B. Make a more detailed outline. The paragraph outline below will help you.

Paragraph Outline

_____ for several
reasons. The first reason is _____
_____ . (Supporting fact) _____
_____.
The second reason is _____.
(Supporting fact) _____.
The final reason is _____
_____ . (Supporting fact) _____
_____ . (Concluding sentence) _____
_____.

3. Write a rough draft.

4. Revise your rough draft.

Using the checklist below, check your rough draft or let your partner check it.

Paragraph Checklist

_____ 1. Does your paragraph have a title?

_____ 2. Did you indent the first line?

_____ 3. Did you write on every other line on your paper? (Look at pages 6–7 for instructions on paragraph form.)

_____ 4. Does your paragraph have a topic sentence?

_____ 5. Does your topic sentence have a controlling idea?

_____ 6. Do your sentences support your topic sentence?

_____ 7. Are your ideas in the correct order?

_____ 8. Does your paragraph have a concluding sentence?

5. Edit your paragraph.

Work with a partner or a teacher to edit your paragraph. Correct spelling, punctuation, vocabulary, and grammar.

6. Write your final copy.

Circle the correct answer.

1. How many different kinds of species of insects are living on earth?

   a. One million

   b. Three million

2. How many times its body length can a flea jump?

   a. Twenty times

   b. Sixty times

3. Most animals have changed over the last million years. But cockroaches have not changed in any way for a long time. How long?

   a. Two hundred fifty million years

   b. Fifty million years

4. Some worms have more than one heart. How many hearts can some worms have?

   a. Five hearts

   b. Ten hearts

5. How many stomachs does a honey bee have?

   a. One

   b. Two

6. How many times its body weight can an ant lift?

   a. Fifty times

   b. Ten times

7. Can a fly see in more directions at one time than a human being?

   a. Yes

   b. No

8. What kind of food do flies eat?

   a. Any food

   b. Liquid food

9. How do insects breathe?

    a. Through their mouths

    b. Through their bellies

10. Do fleas have wings?

    a. Yes

    b. No

UNIT 6

WALK NAVY

Inventions

Chapter 11: Crazy Inventions

PRE-READING QUESTIONS

Discuss these questions with your classmates or teacher.

1. What can the object in the picture do?
2. What would you like the object in the picture to do?
3. When do you think we can use objects like these in everyday life?

Reading: Crazy Inventions

Every year the U.S. government records thousands of **inventions**. Of these only a few become popular and make a lot of money. There are thousands of inventions that nobody wants. Here are some of those.

In 1879, somebody invented a new type of "fire escape." This was a special "hat" which had a parachute on top. You **attached** the hat with a **strap** under your chin. With this special hat on you could jump from a building on fire and float **safely** down. With it there was also a special pair of shoes with thick rubber soles, so the person landed safely.

There was a special alarm clock for people who had problems waking up in the morning. This clock had sixty pieces of wood that hung above your head. At the right time, the pieces of wood dropped down on you when you were sleeping. They hit you but did not hurt you. Therefore, you woke up.

Another invention was the bicycle seat to stop a thief. This seat had **needles** in it. When the owner rode the bicycle the needles were down. But when the bicycle was not in use, the needles were up. Therefore, a thief who jumped on the bike got a nice surprise!

VOCABULARY

Complete the definitions with one of the following words.

attach	an invention	soles
strap	needle	safely

1. When somebody makes something which did not exist before, it is

   _____.

2. A narrow band of material such as leather that holds something

   together is a _____.

3. When you do something carefully and without danger, you do it

   _____.

4. The under or bottom parts of your shoes, but not the heels, are

the _____.

5. Before we sew, we put thread through the hole of a

_____.

6. When you join or fix one thing to another you

_____ it.

A. Looking for the Main Ideas

Circle the letter of the correct answer.

1. The U.S. government records _____.
   a. only a few inventions
   b. thousands of inventions
   c. only inventions that nobody wants

2. For people who had problems waking up, somebody invented a special _____.
   a. piece of wood
   b. sleep
   c. alarm clock

3. Another invention was a bicycle seat _____.
   a. to stop a thief
   b. that you could not use
   c. that was not on a bike

B. Looking for Details

Circle T if the sentence is true. Circle F if the sentence is false.

1. The fire escape was a special "hat" and shoes.	T	F
2. The special shoes of the fire escape had parachutes.	T	F
3. You attached the shoes to your chin.	T	F
4. The special alarm clock had sixty clocks.	T	F
5. The special alarm clock hung over your head.	T	F
6. The bicycle seat to stop a thief had needles.	T	F

DISCUSSION

1. Why do people invent things?
2. What is your favorite invention? Why is it useful?
3. Make a list of all the inventions you use.

WRITING

Read the following paragraph written by a student.

Model Paragraph

My Answering Machine

I got an answering machine for my birthday and I soon realized what a useful machine this is. I am not home most of the day, so someone can leave a message and I call them back. There is no way they can say they can't get in touch with you. Sometimes when I am home and have work to do, the phone never stops. Now I put the machine on. I am not disturbed; therefore, I can do more work. There are some people I just do not want to talk to. Therefore, I put the machine on and I don't have to speak to them. In conclusion, I really do not know how I lived without this wonderful invention.

ORGANIZING

Cause and Effect Paragraph

In Unit Five we looked at **because**, which gave us the reason for or cause of something. In this lesson we will look at the **effect** of something.

First, we must see the difference between the **cause** and the **effect**. The following examples will show the cause and the effect. Notice that an effect can have several causes.

Examples:

1. Mary was late to work. **(Effect)**
   She said her alarm clock does not work. **(Cause)**

2. This machine does not work. **(Effect)**
   It is not plugged in. **(Cause)**

3. There are no computers in our school. **(Effect)**
   The school does not have money to buy them. **(Cause)**
   There is no room in the school to put them. **(Cause)**
   Most of our teachers do not like computers. **(Cause)**

Say which statement is the cause and which is the effect.

1. _effect_ This light is out.

   cause There is no light bulb.

2. _____ The telephone does not work.

   _____ The storm last night pulled the lines down.

3. _____ I forgot to put batteries in it.

   _____ My portable radio does not work.

4. _____ The flight from Canada is three hours late.

   _____ There is a snowstorm in Canada.

5. _____ I cannot see well with these old glasses.

   _____ I need to have my eyes tested again.

6. _____ The typewriter needs a new ribbon.

   _____ There is no writing when I type.

So and *Therefore*

Look at the model paragraph. Underline the words so and therefore. Both these words introduce effect clauses. Now look at the punctuation used with these words. Circle the punctuation before and after these words.

Example:

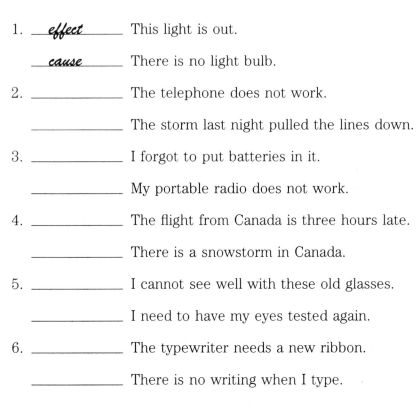

I am not disturbed { , **so** / ; **therefore,** / . **Therefore,** } I can do more work.

So and **therefore** have the same meaning, but **therefore** is more formal.

Punctuate these sentences with a comma where necessary.

1. Mr. Jones has a hearing problem; therefore, he wears a hearing aid.
2. Janet does not like to wear her glasses so she is wearing contact lenses.

3. Peter bought an expensive car. Therefore, he had to get a car alarm.

4. John got a photo copier for his office so he does not have to rush to the copy store every day.

5. Kathy always has her answering machine on; therefore, you can leave a message tonight.

6. Tony hates to wash dishes so he bought a dishwasher.

Exercise 3

Choose the best clause from the list below to complete each sentence.

I am not home during the day	His phone is out of order
My alarm clock does not work	I studied in the language lab all last semester
Typing is not so important for most office jobs today	My eyesight is not so good in the dark

1. _____;

therefore, there is a busy signal on his phone all the time.

2. _____,

so I got up late.

3. _____.

Therefore, I drive very carefully at night.

4. _____,

so I leave my answering machine on.

5. _____;

therefore, I am learning to use a computer.

6. _____.

Therefore, my English pronunciation is much better.

Choose one of the topics below:

1. A great invention (microwave oven/fax machine, etc.)
2. An object that I want to invent
3. An invention that I don't like

1. Pre-writing.

Work with a partner, a group, or alone.

1. Write down the topic at the top of your paper.

2. Think of as many causes and effects about the topic as you can. Write down every word or phrase that comes to your mind.

3. Write your ideas in any order you like. Don't worry if the idea is important or not. Write it down.

2. Develop an outline.

A. The next step is to organize your ideas.

Step 1: *Write the main idea sentence.*

Step 2: *Pick three of the best causes and effects from the ones you wrote.*

Step 3: *Remember to use the words* **so** *and* **therefore**.

B. Make a more detailed outline. The paragraph outline below will help you.

Paragraph Outline

(Topic sentence) _____

(Cause 1) _____ ,

so (effect) _____

(Cause 2) _____ .

Therefore, (effect) _____ .

(Cause 3) _____ ;

therefore, (Effect) _____

(Concluding sentence) _____ .

3. Write a rough draft.

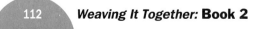

4. Revise your rough draft.

Using the checklist below, check your rough draft or let your partner check it.

Paragraph Checklist

_____ 1. Does your paragraph have a title?

_____ 2. Did you indent the first line?

_____ 3. Did you write on every other line of your paper?

_____ 4. Does your paragraph have a topic sentence?

_____ 5. Does your topic sentence have a controlling idea?

_____ 6. Do your sentences support your topic sentence?

_____ 7. Are your ideas in the correct order?

_____ 8. Does your paragraph have a concluding sentence?

5. Edit your paragraph.

Work with a partner or a teacher to edit your paragraph. Correct spelling, punctuation, vocabulary, and grammar.

6. Write your final copy.

Chapter 12: Robots: Mr. Leachim, Fourth Grade Teacher

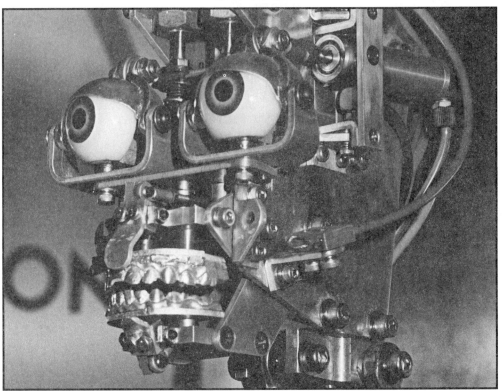

PRE-READING QUESTIONS

Discuss these questions with your classmates or teacher.

1 Would you like a robot to work for you? Give reasons.

2 How can a robot be useful in a school?

3 Can a robot help you teach this class?

Reading: Robots: Mr. Leachim, Fourth-Grade Teacher

Robots are **smart**. With their computer brains, they help people work in dangerous places or do difficult jobs. Some robots do regular jobs. Bobby, the robot mail carrier, brings mail to a large office building in Washington, D.C. He is one of 250 robot mail carriers in the United States. There is also Mr. Leachim, the robot fourth-grade teacher.

Mr. Leachim, who weighs two hundred pounds and is six feet tall, has some advantages as a teacher. One advantage is that he does not forget details. He knows each child's name, the parents' names, and what each child knows and needs to know. In addition, he knows each child's **pets** and hobbies. Mr. Leachim does not make mistakes. Each child goes and tells him his or her name, then **dials** an identification number. His computer brain puts the child's voice and number together. He **identifies** the child with no mistakes. Then he starts the lesson.

Another advantage is that Mr. Leachim is **flexible**. If the children need more time to do their lessons they can move **switches**. In this way they can repeat Mr. Leachim's lesson over and over again. When the children do a good job, he tells them something interesting about their hobbies. At the end of the lesson the children switch Mr. Leachim off.

VOCABULARY

Complete the sentences. Circle the letter of the correct answer.

1. Animals that you like very much and keep at home are

   _____.

   a. hobbies

   b. pets

2. A person who can change from what he/she usually does is

   _____.

   a. regular

   b. flexible

3. A person who is intelligent is _____.

   a. smart

   b. tall

4. When you push buttons with numbers or letters on them like on a telephone, you _____.

    a. dial

    b. forget

5. When you turn a light on or off, you flip a _____.

    a. switch

    b. screen

6. When you can name somebody, or tell who somebody is, you can _____ that person.

    a. move

    b. identify

COMPREHENSION

A. Looking for the Main Ideas

Circle the letter of the best answer.

1. Robots _____.

    a. can help people in regular jobs

    b. cannot help people do difficult jobs

    c. only carry mail

2. Mr. Leachim is a _____.

    a. mail carrier robot

    b. fourth-grade teacher

    c. fourth-grade teacher robot

3. Mr. Leachim has _____.

    a. some advantages

    b. no advantages

    c. one hobby

B. Looking for Details

Circle T if the sentence is true. Circle F if the sentence is false.

1. Bobby is a robot mail carrier in an office building.	T	F
2. There are 250 robot mail carriers in the United States.	T	F
3. Mr. Leachim identifies a child by her/his voice only.	T	F
4. Mr. Leachim does not know each child's name.	T	F

5. Mr. Leachim knows each child's pets and hobbies.   T   F

6. When the lesson is over, the child dials an identification   T   F
number.

DISCUSSION

Discuss these questions with your classmates.

1. Discuss what you want robots of the future to do.

2. List four advantages (good things) about a robot teacher and four
disadvantages (bad things).

WRITING

Read the following paragraph written by a student.

Model Paragraph

A Robot Teacher

    In my opinion, you can get some advantages if you have a
robot to teach you English. First of all, you feel at ease and
relaxed. When you make a mistake, you are not embarrassed.
Second, the student is in control. You can ask the robot to repeat
something over and over again. But you cannot ask your teacher
to do that. In addition, learning with a robot is like a game. It is
fun, but learning with a teacher is usually not like a game. In
conclusion, a robot teacher makes you feel at ease, in control, and
you have fun.

ORGANIZING

Advantages and Disadvantages

*The paragraph above tells us the advantages (the good sides) of
something. It is organized in this way:*

(Topic sentence)

First of all, . . .

or

First, . . .

The first advantage is . . .

(+ supporting sentence)

Second, . . .

or

The second advantage is . . .

(+ supporting sentence)

In addition,. . .

or

Moreover,. . .

(+ supporting sentence)

In conclusion,. . .

Read the model paragraph *again. How many advantages are there?*

Fact or Opinion?

Now look at the topic sentence of the model paragraph. The student gives us a statement of opinion. It is not a fact. A statement of fact gives information that everyone thinks is true. Opinions tell us what one person thinks is true. Other people may have different opinions.

Exercise 1

Are the statements below facts or opinions? Circle the correct answer.

1. You feel at ease and relaxed with a robot teacher.

    Fact   Opinion

2. There are some 250 robot mail carriers in the United States.

    Fact   Opinion

3. With a robot teacher the student is in control.

    Fact   Opinion

4. Mr. Leachim, the robot teacher, weighs two hundred pounds and is six feet tall.

    Fact   Opinion

5. Learning with a robot is like a game.

    Fact   Opinion

If your statement is an opinion, you can start with one of the following:

In my opinion, . . .

I believe. . .

I think. . .

I feel. . .

After you give an opinion you must support it with facts and/or examples.

Transitions Showing Addition:
In Addition and *Moreover*

When you give a list of advantages, reasons, or other ideas in a paragraph, you can use transitions which show addition. Transitions like **in addition** and **moreover** show addition. **In addition** and **moreover** have the same meaning.

> First (of all), . . .
>
> Second, . . .
>
> **In addition**, . . .
>
> **Moreover**, . . .
>
> Finally, . . .

In addition *and* moreover *are not always at the beginning of the sentence. Look at the examples below and note the punctuation with each.*

Examples:

> **In addition**, he knows each child's pets and hobbies.
>
> He knows, **in addition**, each child's pets and hobbies.
>
> **Moreover**, he knows each child's pets and hobbies.
>
> He knows, **moreover**, each child's pets and hobbies.

Now underline the transition that shows addition in the model paragraph. Circle the punctuation marks before and after the transition words.

Exercise 2

In the sentences below, in addition *and* moreover *are used in the middle of the sentence. Rewrite the sentences. Put the words* in addition *and* moreover *at the beginning of the sentences. Use the correct punctuation.*

1. The robot CORA was a brain on wheels. CORA, in addition, could recharge her own batteries.

   _____

   _____

2. The Brave Cop robot can disarm bombs. Brave Cop, moreover, can shoot with his gun.

   _____

   _____

3. The Security Guard robot finds the enemy with his special sensors. The Security Guard, in addition, uses high sounds to hurt the enemy.

_____

_____

4. DA II, the Robot Maid, can do all kinds of jobs in the house. DA II, moreover, can do jobs in the yard.

_____

_____

5. The robot AROK can do many things in the home, like vacuum, take out the trash, and bring in the mail. AROK, in addition, can tell jokes.

_____

_____

6. Beetle, the Robot Truck, can break down walls. Beetle, moreover, can be very gentle.

_____

_____

WRITING PRACTICE

Choose one of the topics below:
1. The disadvantages of a robot teacher
2. The advantages OR disadvantages of a robot security guard
3. The advantages OR disadvantages of a robot astronaut

1. Pre-writing.

Work with a partner, a group, or alone.

1. Write down the topic at the top of your paper.
2. Think of as many reasons to support your opinion as possible. Remember to choose only *one* side: advantage or disadvantage.
3. Which of these reasons can you support with facts or examples?

2. Develop an outline.

A. Organize your ideas.

Step 1: *Write the topic sentence, which tells the reader your position on the subject (Advantages or Disadvantages of . . .). If it is an opinion, use the words: "In my opinion,. . ." or "I believe . . ." etc.*

Step 2: *Pick three supporting reasons for your opinion. Make sure these reasons are different from each other, and that you can write a supporting sentence (fact or personal example) for each.*

Step 3: *Remember to signal each reason.*

B. Make a more detailed outline. The paragraph outline below will help you.

Paragraph Outline

(Topic sentence) _____.
(First advantage/disadvantage) _____.
(Supporting sentence) _____.
(Second advantage/disadvantage) _____..
(Supporting sentence) _____.
In addition, (Third advantage/disadvantage) _____.
(Supporting sentence) _____.
(Concluding sentence) _____.

---

3. Write a rough draft.

4. Revise your rough draft.

Using the checklist below, check your rough draft or let your partner check it.

Paragraph Checklist

_____ 1. Does your paragraph have a title?

_____ 2. Did you indent the first line?

_____ 3. Did you write on every other line of the paper?

_____ 4. Does your paragraph have a topic sentence?

_____ 5. Does your topic sentence have a controlling idea?

_____ 6. Do your reasons support your topic sentence?

_____ 7. Are your ideas in the correct order?

_____ 8. Does your paragraph have a concluding sentence?

5. Edit your paragraph.

Work with a partner or a teacher to edit your paragraph. Correct spelling, punctuation, vocabulary, and grammar.

6. Write your final copy.

Test your knowledge. Circle the correct answer.

1. Who invented the electric light bulb?
    a. Thomas Alva Edison
    b. Albert Einstein
    c. Marie Curie

2. A thermos bottle keeps hot drinks hot and cold drinks cool. The word *thermos* is Greek. It means _____.
    a. hot
    b. cold
    c. temperature

3. In 1876 Alexander Graham Bell said to his assistant, "Watson, come here. I want you." What was the invention?
    a. The telegraph
    b. Television
    c. The telephone

4. Alexander Fleming discovered penicillin in 1929. What nationality was he?
    a. German
    b. Scottish
    c. American

5. We name this popular food after this person. He loved to play cards. One day he got hungry but did not want to leave the game. He told his servants to bring him some meat between two slices of bread. He was the Earl of _____.
    a. Hamburger
    b. Deli
    c. Sandwich

6. A kind of stove and bifocal eyeglasses were the inventions of a famous American statesman. Who was he?
    a. George Washington
    b. Benjamin Franklin
    c. Abraham Lincoln

7. John Baird (1888–1946) was a Scottish inventor. What was his famous invention?

    a. Television

    b. Color photography

    c. The vacuum cleaner

8. The Nobel Prize, a special prize for people who work for peace in the world, is named after Alfred Nobel. Alfred Nobel invented

_____.

    a. radium

    b. radar

    c. dynamite

UNIT 7

The Law

Chapter 13: It's the Law!

PRE-READING QUESTIONS

Discuss these questions with your classmates or teacher.

1. Do you think there are too many laws?

2. What do you think is a very bad law in North America? Give reasons.

3. What do you think is a very good law? Give reasons.

Reading: It's the Law

It's the law, but which law? **Federal** or state law? In the United States there are different **layers** of laws. At the top is federal law, which Congress makes for all people in the United States. Then each state makes laws about things in its own territory. The laws that each state makes must not go against federal laws. **Counties** and towns also make **rules**. A town may require that you have a **license** for your bicycle, for example.

Here are some similarities and differences in state laws. In California children must go to school from age seven to sixteen. However, in the state of Oregon they must go to school from age seven to eighteen. Similarly, there are differences in how you get a driver's license. In California you can get a regular driver's license, without driver education, at age eighteen. In contrast, in Colorado you must be twenty-one.

Some states have a number of very special old laws. Most people have never heard of these laws. Nobody **gets arrested** for breaking them, but they are still "laws." For example, in Kentucky, everybody must have a bath at least once a year. In Indiana you cannot travel on a bus less than four hours after you eat garlic. In California it is against the law to enter a restaurant on horseback.

VOCABULARY

Complete the definitions. Circle the letter of the correct answer.

1. In the United States laws which are of the central government and not of each state are _____.
   - a. federal
   - b. town

2. A large piece of land, which is part of a state and which can have its own laws, is called a _____.
   - a. congress
   - b. county

3. When you want to use English grammar correctly, you must follow these _____.
   - a. rules
   - b. laws

4. A card or piece of paper which gives you official permission to do something like drive is called a _____.

    a. license

    b. state

5. When the police come and take someone in the name of the law, the person gets _____.

    a. arrested

    b. a license

6. When things lie between or on top of something else, they are in

_____.

    a. schools

    b. layers

COMPREHENSION

A. Looking for the Main Ideas

Circle the letter of the correct answer.

1. In the United States there _____.

    a. is only one law

    b. are only state laws

    c. are different layers of laws

2. Each state makes its _____.

    a. own laws

    b. laws the same as California's

    c. laws for driver's licenses only

3. Some states have old laws that _____.

    a. everyone gets arrested for

    b. are very special

    c. are not really laws anymore

B. Looking for Details

Circle T if the sentence is true. Circle F if the sentence is false.

1. Each state can make laws against federal laws.   T F
2. A town can make its own rules.   T F
3. In California children must go to school until they are eighteen.   T F
4. In Colorado you must be twenty-one to get a driver's license.   T F
5. In Oregon you must start school at age six.   T F
6. In Kentucky you must have a bath at least once a year.   T F

DISCUSSION

Discuss these questions with your classmates.

1. At what age can you get a driver's license in your country? How long must you attend school?
2. Which laws do you think should be changed in your country?
3. Do you know any strange laws in your country or another country?
4. Discuss the rules and regulations you had in your school in your country. Then list three things that are different from your present school. List three things that are the same.

Now read the following paragraph written by a student. What country does the student come from?

Model Paragraph

Classroom Behavior Rules

There are some similarities and differences in the classroom behavior rules between North America and my country, X. First, there is the student's right to speak. In my language class in North America students can ask the teacher questions. They can even ask questions when the teacher is giving a lesson. Similarly, in my country students have the right to ask questions. However, they can only ask questions at the end of the class. Next, students respect their teachers. In North America students look up to teachers and respect them. For example, when the teacher asks them to speak they must look into the teacher's eyes to show respect. Likewise, in my country, X, students respect teachers; however, when a teacher asks us to speak we look down to show respect. We do not look into their eyes. In conclusion, there are both similarities and differences in the way students behave toward their teachers in the classroom.

ORGANIZING

Comparing and Contrasting

In this unit you will learn how to organize a compare and contrast paragraph.

When we **compare** we look at the similarities between two things, two people, two ideas, etc. When we **contrast**, we look at the differences.

There are two ways of organizing your paragraph when you compare and contrast. The following are outlines (Plan A and Plan B) of the two ways you can organize your compare and contrast paragraph.

Look at the outlines and then look at the model paragraph just given.
Which outline does it follow, Plan A or Plan B? How many similarities
can you see in the model paragraph? How many differences can you
see in the model paragraph?

Plan A

Topic sentence
  I. Similarities: North America and my country
     A. The right to speak
     B. Respect for teacher
 II. Differences: North America and my country
     A. The right to speak
     B. Respect for teacher
Concluding sentence

Plan B

Topic sentence
  I. The right to speak
     A. Similarities: North America and my country
     B. Differences: North America and my country
 II. Respect for teacher
     A. Similarities: North America and my country
     B. Differences: North America and my country
Concluding sentence

Transitions Showing Contrast: *However*

However connects an idea in the first sentence with a contrasting idea in the
second sentence. **However** tells the reader that an idea opposite from the
first sentence will follow. **However** has the same meaning as **but**. **However**
is used mostly in formal writing. Notice the punctuation used with **however**.
Both the following examples have the same meaning.

Examples:

In California children go to school until age sixteen; **however**, in
Oregon they go to school until age eighteen.

In California children go to school until age sixteen. **However**, in
Oregon they go to school until age eighteen.

Now underline the transition however *in the reading passage and in*
the model paragraph. Next, look at the punctuation with however*. Go*
back and circle all the punctuation marks with however*.*

Connect the following sentences with **however.** *Use* **however** *with both kinds of punctuation.*

1. In California you can get a driver's license at age eighteen. In Colorado you must be twenty-one.

   _____

   _____

2. In the United States students in high school do not wear uniforms. In my country students must wear uniforms.

   _____

   _____

3. In most countries people drive on the right. In Great Britain and Australia people drive on the left.

   _____

   _____

4. In North America letter grades are given in high school. In my country numbers 1 to 10 are given.

   _____

   _____

Transitions Showing Similarity: *Similarly* and *Likewise*

Similarly and **likewise** connect an idea in the first sentence with a similar idea in the second sentence. **Similarly** or **likewise** introduces the second sentence. Use a comma after **similarly** or **likewise**.

Example:

In North America students can ask the teacher questions.
Likewise, ⎱ in my country students have the right
Similarly, ⎰ to ask the teacher questions.

Connect the following sentences with **similarly** *or* **likewise**. *Use the correct punctuation.*

1. Students in the United States respect their teachers. In my country students respect their teachers.

   _____

   _____

2. In California you must attend school until age sixteen. In Alaska, Colorado, Arizona, and Florida you must attend until you are sixteen.

   _____

   _____

3. A driver in a car must wear a seat belt. The passenger next to the driver must wear a seat belt.

   _____

   _____

4. You may not vote until you are eighteen. Before you are eighteen, you cannot write a will or make a contract.

   _____

WRITING PRACTICE

Compare and contrast one of the topics below:

1. Traffic laws/regulations in your country and North America (or another country)
2. Past and present class/school rules
3. Police officers in your country and North America (or another country)

1. Pre-writing.

Work with a partner, a group, or alone.

1. Write the topic at the top of your paper.
2. Think of as many similarities as you can. Write them down.
3. Think of as many differences as you can. Write them down.

2. Develop an outline.

A. Organize your ideas.

Step 1: *Write your topic sentence.*

Example:

There are some interesting similarities and differences in traffic laws between North America and my country, X.

Step 2: *Name two things that make them similar.*

1. _____

2. _____

Name two things that make them different.

1. _____

2. _____

Step 3: *Can you write at least one supporting sentence for each of the similarities and differences above? If you can't find good examples, you may have to change your points.*

Step 4: *Remember the compare and contrast transitions:* **however, likewise, similarly.** *Think of where you can put these in your paragraph.*

B. Make a more detailed outline. The paragraph outline below will help you.

Paragraph Outline

(Topic sentence) _____.
(Similarity 1) _____.
(Supporting sentence) _____.
(Similarity 2) _____.
(Supporting sentence) _____.
(Difference 1) _____.
(Supporting sentence) _____.
(Difference 2) _____.
(Supporting sentence) _____.
(Concluding sentence) _____.

3. Write a rough draft.

4. Revise your rough draft.

Using the checklist below, check your rough draft or let your partner check it.

Paragraph Checklist

_____ 1. Does your paragraph have a title?

_____ 2. Did you indent the first line?

_____ 3. Did you write on every other line of the paper?

_____ 4. Does your paragraph have a topic sentence?

_____ 5. Does your topic sentence have a controlling idea?

_____ 6. Do your similarities and differences support your topic sentence?

_____ 7. Are your ideas in the correct order?

_____ 8. Does your paragraph have a concluding sentence?

5. Edit your paragraph.

Work with a partner or a teacher to edit your paragraph. Correct spelling, punctuation, vocabulary, and grammar.

6. Write your final copy.

Chapter 14: Laws About Children

PRE-READING QUESTIONS

Discuss these questions with your classmates or teacher.

1. Do you think these children are unhappy?

2. Do you think this can happen today?

Reading: Laws About Children

In general, laws for children are a good thing. One hundred years ago in **industrial** countries, children worked eighteen hours a day in a factory at age seven. The factory owner could **beat** a child who fell asleep or was not fast enough. Both parents and teachers could do the same.

Today, there are many laws about children all over the world. Some people think children must obey rules and be **punished**. Other people do not agree. The Inuits, or Eskimos, in Alaska almost never punish their children. The parents do not hit them. If the children **go too far**, the parents punish them by **making fun of** them.

Children in other parts of the world are not as lucky as Eskimo children. American parents can **spank** their children at home, but a teacher cannot hit a child in a public school. This is also true in Germany. In contrast, in Sweden it is against the law for anyone to hit a child. Swedish parents cannot spank their children. The children also have a special government official (an ombudsman) who works for their rights. There is even a plan for children to divorce their parents, though this is not a law—yet!

VOCABULARY

Complete the definitions with the words below.

spank	make fun of	beat
industrial	punish	go too far

1. When you hit someone again and again with a lot of strength, you

   _____ the person.

2. A country where there are factories where many people work

   using machines to make things is _____.

3. When you laugh at someone in a way that is not kind, you

   _____ the person.

4. When you hit a child with an open hand, usually on its behind, you

   _____ the child.

5. When you go against the law, the government makes you pay a
   fine or go to prison to _____ you.

6. When you do more than is acceptable, you _____.

COMPREHENSION

A. Looking for the Main Ideas

Circle the letter of the correct answer.

1. Laws for children are _____.
   a. not a good idea
   b. a good thing
   c. only for parents

2. Today there are laws about _____.
   a. children in North America only
   b. making fun of children in Alaska
   c. children all over the world

3. In North America _____.
   a. parents can spank their children
   b. teachers can hit children
   c. parents cannot hit children

B. Looking for Details

*One word in each sentence is not correct. Cross out the word and
write the correct word above it.*

1. Eskimos almost never divorce their children.
2. In Sweden children have an owner who works for their rights.
3. A teacher cannot hit a child in a special school in North America.
4. In Germany it is against the law to hit a child.
5. In Sweden parents cannot help their children.
6. Eskimo parents punish teachers by making fun of them.

Discuss these questions with your classmates.

1. Discuss why it is good or bad for a parent to hit a child.

2. Do you think that teachers in schools should have the right to hit a child?

3. Explain how children are punished at home or at school in your country. Say why it is good or bad.

4. List three similarities and three differenes between your past and present teachers.

WRITING

Read the following paragraph written by a student.

Model Paragraph

Two English Teachers

There are both some similarities and differences between my old English teacher in X and my present English teacher in the United States. Both my English teachers controlled the class well. If a student made trouble in the classroom, we were all responsible and had extra work. This made the student unpopular and nobody wanted to be unpopular. Both my teacher back home and my present teacher know their subject well. They both made sure we knew the rules of the language very well. Although both my teachers had these similarities, they also had differences on these same points. When a student was always troublesome in class my old teacher would go to the parents because my school was small and there was no principal. In contrast, my present teacher sends the troublesome student to a counselor. The counselor then sends the student to the assistant principal and so on. Also, the way my two teachers taught English is different. My teacher back home taught us a rule of grammar and then gave examples. In contrast, my present teacher gives us examples first. If we need a rule we work it out from the examples. In conclusion, both my English teachers with their similarities and differences were excellent teachers.

Comparing and Contrasting

Look at the outlines for compare and contrast paragraphs (Plan A and Plan B) on page 131. Which outline does the model paragraph above follow?

How many similarities can you see in the model paragraph? How many differences can you see in the model paragraph?

Transitions Showing Contrast: *In contrast*

In this unit we looked at the transition **however** to show contrast. **In contrast** is another transition we can use to show contrast. Notice the punctuation with **in contrast.**

Example:

My teacher back home taught us a rule of grammar and then gave examples. **In contrast**, my present teacher gives us examples first.

Now go back to the model paragraph and underline where you see the transition in contrast. *Then circle the punctuation marks before and after it.*

Exercise 1

Rewrite the sentences below using in contrast *in the second sentence and the correct punctuation.*

1. Parents can hit their children in North America. In Sweden nobody

   can hit a child.

   _____

   _____

2. Teachers in public schools in North America cannot hit a child.

   Teachers in private schools can hit a child.

   _____

   _____

3. One hundred years ago there were no laws for children in North America. Today, there are hundreds of laws.

_____

_____

4. Teachers in my country are very serious. Teachers in North America are friendly.

_____

_____

5. In my country a teacher could hit a child in school. In North America a teacher in a public school cannot hit a child.

_____

_____

Using *Both . . . and* for Similarities

When two things or two people have something in common, we use **both . . . and**. These words always go together. They are a paired conjunction. The word after **both** must be the same part of speech (noun, adjective, verb, etc.) as the word after **and**.

Examples:

> **Both** parents **and** teachers could beat a child.
>   (Pl. noun)   (Pl. noun)

> **Both** my teacher back home **and** my present teacher know their subject well.

> My teacher is **both** kind **and** intelligent.
>   (Adj.)   (Adj.)

Now underline all the uses of both . . . and in the model paragraph. Look at the words that follow both . . . and. Are they the same parts of speech?

***Rewrite the two sentences in one sentence using* both . . . and.**

1. In my country parents can spank their children. In North America parents can spank their children.

    Both in my country and in North America parents can spank

    their children.

2. There are similarities in the classroom. There are differences in the classroom.

    _____

    _____

3. The Eskimos do not hit their children. The Swedes do not hit their children.

    _____

    _____

4. My teacher knows her subject. My teacher controls the class well.

    _____

    _____

5. Children who worked in the factories were tired. Children who worked in the factories were unhappy.

    _____

    _____

Compare and contrast one of the topics below:
1. Two teachers
2. The childhood of your mother/father and your childhood
3. Two parents

....

1. Pre-writing.

Work with a partner, a group, or alone.

1. Write the topic at the top of your paper.

2. Write down as many similarities as you can.

3. Write down as many differences as you can.

2. Develop an outline.

A. Organize your ideas.

Step 1: *Write your topic sentence*

Example:

Both my mother and I had interesting childhoods which were similar in many ways yet different.

Step 2: *Write two things that make them similar.*

1. _____

2. _____

Write two things that make them different.

1. _____

2. _____

Step 3: *Make sure you have at least one good supporting sentence for each of the above points.*

Step 4: *Remember the compare and contrast transitions:* **however, in contrast, likewise, similarly, both . . . and.** *Think of where you can use these in your paragraph.*

Step 5: *Which paragraph outline do you want to use, Plan A or Plan B?*

B. Make a more detailed outline. You can use the outline below or the other outline in this unit to help you.

Paragraph Outline

(Topic Sentence) _____ .
(Point 1) _____ .
(Similarity) _____ .
(Supporting sentence) _____ .
(Difference) _____ .
(Supporting sentence) _____ .
(Point 2) _____ .
(Similarity) _____ .
(Supporting sentence) _____ .
(Difference) _____ .
(Supporting sentence) _____ .
(Concluding sentence) _____ .

(If you want to, you can try *three* points of comparison and contrast or *three* similarities and differences.)

This will be the last paragraph you will write in this book. The paragraph should be about 150–200 words.

3. Write a rough draft.

4. Revise your rough draft.

Using the checklist below, check your rough draft or let your partner check it.

Paragraph Checklist

_____ 1. Does your paragraph have a title?

_____ 2. Did you indent the first line?

_____ 3. Does your paragraph have a topic sentence?

_____ 4. Does your topic sentence have a controlling idea?

_____ 5. Do your similarities and differences support your topic sentence?

_____ 6. Are your ideas in the correct order?

_____ 7. Does your paragraph have a concluding sentence?

5. Edit your paragraph.

Work with a partner or a teacher to edit your paragraph. Correct spelling, punctuation, vocabulary, and grammar.

6. Write your final copy.

Test yourself. Check True or False.

1. In Sweden you must drive with your car headlights on all the time.
   True   False

2. In Germany there is no law for how fast you can drive on the
   freeway (Autobahn).
   True   False

3. You can be fined $300 if you pick a wildflower anywhere in the
   United States.
   True   False

4. The minimum age for buying alcohol in the United States is
   twenty.
   True   False

5. From all the levels of government, federal, state, and local,
   Americans get 150 new laws each year.
   True   False

6. From all the levels of government, federal, state, and local,
   Americans get two million new regulations every year.
   True   False

7. The age of majority, the age at which a person has legal control over
   his actions, is eighteen in forty-seven of the fifty states in the United
   States.
   True   False